Stained Glass
in the
Garden

Stained Glass
in the
Garden

Vicki Payne

Sterling Publishing Co., Inc.
New York

Prolific Impressions Production Staff:

Editor in Chief: Mickey Baskett
Copy Editor: Phyllis Mueller
Graphics: Karen Turpin
Styling: Lenos Key
Photography: Jerry Mucklow
Administration: Jim Baskett

Library of Congress Cataloging-in-Publication Data Available

Payne, Vicki.
  Stained glass in the garden / Vicki Payne.
       p. cm.
  Includes index.
  ISBN-13: 978-1-4027-3506-6
  ISBN-10: 1-4027-3506-5
1. Garden ornaments and furniture. 2. Garden structures. 3. Glass craft. I. Title.
SB473.5.P39 2007
684.1'8--dc22

2006038779

2 4 6 8 10 9 7 5 3 1

Published by Sterling Publishing Co., Inc.
387 Park Avenue South, New York, NY 10016
© 2007 by Prolific Impressions, Inc.
Distributed in Canada by Sterling Publishing
c/o Canadian Manda Group, 165 Dufferin Street,
Toronto, Ontario, Canada M6K 3H6
Distributed in the United Kingdom by GMC Distribution Services,
Castle Place, 166 High Street, Lewes, East Sussex, England BN7 1XU
Distributed in Australia by Capricorn Link (Australia) Pty. Ltd.
P.O. Box 704, Windsor, NSW 2756, Australia

Printed in China
All rights reserved

ISBN-13: 978-1-4027-3506-6
ISBN-10: 1-4027-3506-5

For information about custom editions, special sales, premium and corporate purchases, please contact Sterling Special Sales Department at 800-805-5489 or specialsales@sterlingpub.com.

About
Vicki Payne

Vicki Payne is an internationally recognized craft and home improvement expert and host of two national television series, *For Your Home* and *Glass with Vicki Payne*. She has established herself as one of the craft industry's most successful and respected entrepreneurs. As CEO of Cutters Productions, she has produced thousands of how-to videos in more than seventeen years of quality television programming, including five national weekly series and dozens of successful fundraisers for public television. Cutters Productions received awards for "Best Performing Pledge Specials" in 2003 and 2004 and won the 2005 MVP award from American Public Television.

Cutters Productions' series and specials are carried by more than 284 public television stations, the Create Channel, and American Life TV on cable throughout the United States. The shows include *For Your Home, Paint, Paper and Crafts, Glass with Vicki Payne, Kid Concoctions,* and *The Donna Dewberry Show.* Vicki is a frequent and popular guest on a number of programs airing on HGTV and The Discovery Channel and on home improvement and crafting shows. She hosted the DIY Network's Crafting series and, with her daughter Sloan Rutter, hosts the Handmade Gifts Workshops on the DIY Network.

In addition to her work in television, Vicki is an accomplished writer, speaker, and educator. Her work is frequently published in shelter, craft, and trade magazines. She is the author of a number of books about stained glass,

including *Stained Glass in an Afternoon* (Sterling, 2002), *Traditional Leaded Glass Crafting* (Sterling, 2003), *The Stained Glass Classroom* (Sterling, 2004), and *Easy Home Organizer* (Sterling, 2006). She is an executive board member of the Art Glass Association and a member of the Craft and Hobby Association and Women in the Home Furnishing Industry.

Page 25

Page 48

Table of Contents

The Copper Foil Method

Copper Foil Projects

Page 68

Page 93

Page 109

Bring Stained Glass to Your Garden

Stained glass, with its endless variety of textures, patterns, and iridized finishes, has captured my interest as an artist for over 25 years. Every time I see a new piece of glass, I can't wait to cut and shape it into a new project.

This book showcases the versatility of glass for crafting projects to use outdoors – in mosaics, stepping stones, panels, and accessories that will add color and beauty to your porch, patio, deck, and garden. You'll learn all about the tools and supplies you need to get started and learn time-honored techniques for making glass and mixed media mosaics. You'll also see how to make panels and three dimensional objects from glass using the copper foil method.

This book includes instructions, photos, and patterns for making more than 30 stained glass projects. Wonderful mosaic table tops. A fabulous fountain. A beautiful blue birdbath. Colorful hanging panels. Decorated flower pots. Candle holders, a luminary, and a lantern. Numerous step-by-step photos that explain the techniques so you can craft with confidence.

Who hasn't admired the beauty of stained glass and marveled at the rich colors, the gorgeous textures, the sparkle of the glass, the soft gleam of metal edging? But maybe you thought stained glass wasn't something you could make – it seemed so difficult, so time-consuming. Think again, relax, and enjoy!

Vicki Payne

Basic Supplies & Tools

Stained Glass

The terms "stained glass" and "art glass" are interchangeable – both are used to describe types of glass manufactured for decorative purposes, as opposed to "flat" or "float" glass, which is commonly used for auto glass, windows, and doors.

There are two basic categories of stained glass: opalescent and cathedral. **Opalescent glass** is glass you cannot easily see through; **cathedral glass** is glass you can see through more clearly. For the past few decades, the most popular type of "stained" glass isn't colored glass – it's clear art glass. Within each category of glass there are unlimited variations and combinations of colors, textures, densities, and patterns.

Glass is sold by the square foot or by the pound. It costs between $2.50 and $7 a square foot, depending on the color of the glass. If you buy glass by the square foot, you get a piece of glass that is 12" x 12". If you buy glass by the pound, you generally get 1-1/2 pounds of glass to the square foot. It is a good rule of thumb to buy about 25 percent more glass than the size of your project; you may use more than you anticipated. "Always buy more" is a good rule of thumb – you can use it for a future project if it's left over. It is always a heartbreaker to go back to the glass shop and discover there is no more of the glass you need in stock and to have to wait for the next shipment to come in.

When choosing glass colors, the best rule of thumb is to buy what you like. If you like pink, use pink. If you like yellow, select yellow. Feel free to change the colors of any of the projects in this book to suit your taste or your decor.

A popular glass color to use is *iridized* glass. The glass surface has been given a treatment of heated metallic oxides that results in an iridescent, rainbow-like metallic effect on the surface. The colors seem to move and change when viewed from different angles.

Other Glass

Stained glass **rondels** are handmade glass circles that have been used for centuries to fashion door and window panels. They come in a wide variety of colors and sizes. They can be used as accents or as central motifs in panels.

Glass nuggets are flat on the back and rounded on the top. They come in a variety of shapes and colors and can be used as accents or as the main pieces for fanciful sculptural designs.

Glass Types & Textures

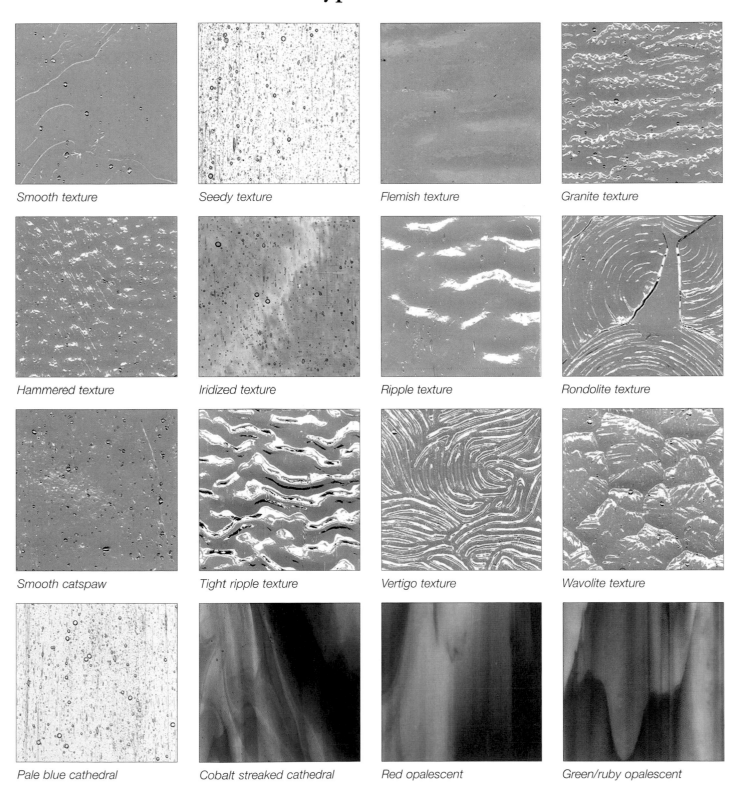

Smooth texture

Seedy texture

Flemish texture

Granite texture

Hammered texture

Iridized texture

Ripple texture

Rondolite texture

Smooth catspaw

Tight ripple texture

Vertigo texture

Wavolite texture

Pale blue cathedral

Cobalt streaked cathedral

Red opalescent

Green/ruby opalescent

Glass Cutting & Breaking Tools

Carbide Glass Cutter

A handheld **carbide cutter** is what you'll use for most of your glass cutting. Carbide cutters come with different handles in a variety of styles and range in price from just a couple of dollars to about $20. The cutting wheels of all glass cutters need to be lubricated with oil, so a **self-oiling cutter** is convenient to use – it automatically lubricates the wheel as you score.

Lubricating Oil

Lubricating oil is necessary to protect the cutting wheel so the glass cutter will last much longer and because a score line which has been lubricated with oil is much easier to break.

If your cutter is not self-oiling, you'll need to saturate a towel with lubricating oil and keep it handy. Pass the wheel of the cutter over the oil-saturated towel before each score.

You can buy lubricating oil or mix your own. I like to use lamp oil.

Combination Breaking/Grozing Pliers

This combination tool can be used both to hold glass for breaking and to gently remove the small pieces of glass that remain after the glass is scored and broken (the process called "grozing"). Combination pliers have curved, serrated jaws.

Running Pliers

Running pliers have curved jaws that exert pressure on each side of a score line, resulting in a straight, clean break along the score line.

Pictured left to right: Glass and mosaic tile cutter, self-oiling pistol-grip carbide glass cutter, breaking pliers.

Mosaic Glass & Tile Cutters

These spring-loaded wheel cutters with handles like pliers are designed specifically for mosaic work. They are used to quickly nip glass into geometric shapes.

Other Options

For cutting thicker, wavy glass, an **electric glass saw** is recommended.

A **strip cutter** is a glass-cutting tool that can be set to a desired width. It will cut straight, parallel, uniform strips of glass again and again. It's especially useful for making boxes.

Pictured above: a glass saw.

How to Use Tools

Caution! Always wear safety glasses to protect your eyes when cutting glass.

1. **Scoring the glass.** Position your carbide glass cutter at the edge of the piece. Pull the wheel of the cutter down the length of the glass to make a score. (The score is the scratch-like line the cutter makes on the surface of the glass.) Note the angle of the glass cutter.

2. **Breaking a large piece.** To break a larger piece of glass, pick it up and put your fingers on each side of the scored line, under the glass with your thumbs on top. Rock your hands up and away from you. The glass will break along the scored line.

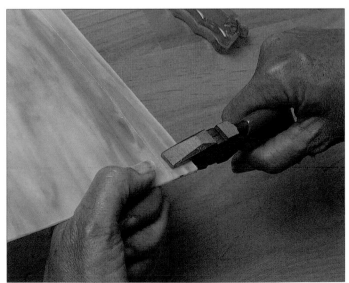

3. **Breaking a smaller piece.** To break a smaller piece of glass such as this narrow strip, hold the glass surface in one hand and the pliers in your other hand. Position the edge of the pliers on the scored line and move the pliers gently to break the glass along the score. (Pliers also work well for breaking curved cuts.)

4. **Nipping smaller pieces.** Mosaic glass and tile cutters can be used to nip small pieces of glass. Hold the glass in one hand and the pliers in the other. Place the cutting edge of the pliers where you want the glass to break and squeeze the handles.

Glass Smoothing Supplies

Glass Grinder

An electric **glass grinder** is a machine with a diamond bit and a tray underneath the bit that contains water. There is a sponge in the back that pumps water up to the bit to keep it wet when you are grinding. The water keeps the dust down and keeps the glass cool so it will not fracture.

A grinder is the fastest, most efficient way to prepare glass pieces and correct problems on the edges of pieces, but grinders are not inexpensive. You might want to check with your local glass shop about renting one. When you use a glass grinder, **always** wear safety glasses and follow the manufacturer's instructions.

Emery Cloth/Carborundum Stone

An **emery cloth** or a **carborundum stone** also may be used to smooth the edges of cut glass pieces. Be forewarned that using a carborundum stone or emery cloth is a slow process, but it's less expensive than buying a grinder.

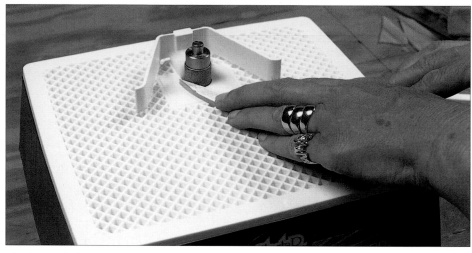

A glass grinder.

Carborundum stone, squares of emery cloth.

Safety Gear

Protective Glasses

Always wear **protective glasses, goggles, or a face shield** when cutting and grinding glass to shield your eyes from glass chips and fragments and splattering flux or solder.

Face Mask

When you are soldering, wear a **face mask** specially designed to protect you from soldering fumes. They are available at stained glass stores and hardware stores. **Always** work in a well-ventilated area when soldering.

Gloves

Making mosaics and working with stained glass can be hard on your hands. Wear rubber, latex, or vinyl gloves when working with grout and work gloves that protect your hands for working with cement. I recommend wearing disposable garden gloves for tinning.

Pattern Making Supplies

Use these supplies to make patterns for cutting out glass pieces and assembling your projects.

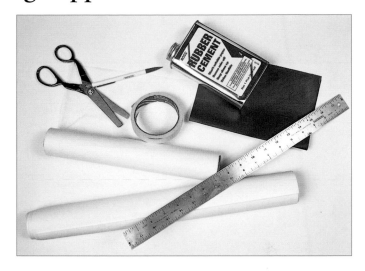

Pattern Paper

I like to use **white bond paper or white craft paper** for patterns, white instead of brown because it is easier to see the colors of colored pencils. If you use a light box for tracing the pattern lines on the glass, white paper is easier to see through.

Tracing Paper & Transfer Paper

Use **tracing paper** and a **pencil** to trace patterns from this (and other) books. Buy tracing paper at crafts and art supply stores.

Use **transfer paper** to transfer designs to pattern paper. You also can use a photocopier to make copies of traced designs.

Colored Pencils

Cutting the pieces for your stained glass projects is easier if you take the time to color in the design with **colored pencils**. That way, you create a color-keyed pattern that's especially helpful when you cut apart the pattern to make templates for cutting.

Ruler

The most important tool you need is a **metal ruler**. An 18" ruler is a good size to have. Make sure it's calibrated from one end all the way to the other. Also make sure it has a cork back. This will prevent it from slipping around while you are drawing and using it to cut glass with.

Pattern Shears

Stained glass is composed of pieces of glass separated by pieces of metal all the way across a project, and the metal takes up space between each piece of glass. When you cut out pattern pieces with **pattern shears** to make templates for cutting your glass, the special blades of the pattern shears (there are three of them) remove a small strip of paper on the cutting lines to allow space for the metal. TIP: Practice cutting with pat-

Pattern shears.

tern shears on some scrap paper before you cut out your pattern to make templates.

Rubber Cement

Use **rubber cement** or a **pattern fixative** to hold pattern pieces in place for cutting and grinding. Either will simply rub off the glass when you're ready to construct your piece. Alternately, you can use two-sided tape or spray adhesive.

Masking Tape

You also need **masking tape** to hold your design in place on your work board and for holding pieces of glass for dimensional projects and boxes together until you solder them. Painter's masking tape is easy to remove.

Markers

To mark on glass, choose markers that aren't permanent on glass and can be rubbed or washed off. Test **felt-tip markers** on a scrap of glass before using. A **china marker**, available at crafts and art supply stores in a variety of colors, is another good choice for marking glass.

Other Supplies

It is a good idea to get a **shoebox** to put your cut-apart pattern pieces in so you don't lose any of them. If you do happen to lose a pattern piece during the process of building your project, you can always make a tracing off your other (un-cut) copy.

Stained Glass Mosaics

Mosaics may look complicated, but mosaic techniques are easy to learn and many mosaic projects are quick and simple to do. Although the most common mosaic material today is tile, many early mosaics were made of glass. The mosaic projects in this book are created by cutting design motifs from glass using the patterns provided. The cut-out motifs are glued on a surface and the areas around the motifs are filled in with randomly placed small pieces of glass. The piece is then grouted – an easy process.
Making a mosaic is a great way to use small scraps of glass left over from other projects.
No soldering is required.

Basic Tools & Supplies

To create glass mosaics, you need these basic tools and supplies:

• **Opalescent glass**, the same type of art glass used for many of the other projects in this book.

• **A surface** to use as a base, such as wood, glass, or terra cotta.

• **An adhesive**, such as white craft glue or silicone adhesive, to hold the glass to the surface.

• **Sanded grout**, to fill the spaces between the pieces of glass, to create a smooth surface, and to add strength and durability.

• **Grout sealer**, to seal the grout and protect it.

• **Tools** – Glass cutting tools, plus some **craft sticks** for applying the adhesive, a **putty knife or spatula or stiff-bristled brush** for applying grout, a **sponge** for wiping grout, and some **soft cloth rags** for polishing.

• **Safety gear**, such as a dust mask and rubber gloves for working with grout, plus safety glasses for cutting glass.

Glass cutting tools, pictured left to right: Mosaic glass and tile cutters, self-oiling pistol-grip carbide glass cutter, breaking pliers.

Grouting supplies, pictured clockwise from top right: Sanded grout powder in a glass mixing bowl, bristle brush, cleaning pad, sponge, glue, protective gloves.

16

Pictured above: Hawaiian Hibiscus Cheese Board. See page 20 for instructions.

Step 1 • Prepare the Pattern

Making Your Own Transfer Paper

Make your own transfer paper to transfer your design to pattern paper by rubbing a pencil with soft lead over the back of your traced design. Position the traced design right side up on pattern paper and go over the lines.

1. Trace the pattern from the book. Enlarge, if needed, using a copy machine or graph paper. Transfer the design to white paper, making two copies.
2. Cut out the pattern pieces from one pattern to make templates for cutting.
3. Transfer the second pattern to the project surface where you'll be assembling the mosaic.

Step 2 • Cut the Glass Pieces

1. Position the pattern pieces on the designated glass colors and trace around the pieces with a marker. Move the glass cutter along the pattern lines on the glass. Cut out the pieces.

2. Use mosaic glass and tile cutters to cut the random shapes that will be used for the background of the mosaic.

Step 3 • Glue the Glass Pieces

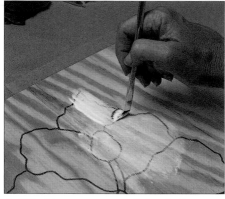

1. Working one area of the design at a time, use a brush to spread glue on the surface.

2. Position the cut glass mosaic pieces over the glue. Let dry.

Step 4 • Grout

1. Mix the Grout

Add liquid to powdered grout and mix according the grout manufacturer's instructions. (A wooden paint stirrer is a good tool for this.) The grout should be thoroughly blended and of a fairly stiff consistency. Mix only as much grout as you think you'll need – you can't save the leftovers.

2. Apply the Grout

Use a stiff-bristle brush (shown here), a craft stick, a putty knife, or a spatula to apply the grout, pressing it into the spaces between the glass pieces. **Don't** use your fingers – the edges of the glass pieces may be sharp. It's a good idea when working with grout to wear rubber, latex, or vinyl gloves – grout is very drying to the skin.

3. Wipe & Polish

When grout has been applied to the entire surface of the tile and has filled all the crevices between the glass pieces, fill a bowl with water, dampen a sponge, and squeeze out the excess water. Wipe the mosaic to remove excess grout from the surface of the glass pieces. Rinse the sponge and wipe again. Repeat until you can see all the pieces though the grout and the grout is smooth and even with the surface of the glass. Let dry.

As the grout dries, a haze will form over the glass. Polish off the haze by rubbing with a soft cloth rag until the glass gleams.

Hawaiian Hibiscus
Serving Tray & Cheese Board
(The Cheese Board is pictured on page 17.)

Every summer my husband Chris and I enjoy hosting a backyard pool party, and we have been collecting colorful Hawaiian-themed party gear for years. This summer I found a great bamboo tray at a discount store. It was an attractive tray, but the bottom was plain so I decided to dress it up with a bright red hibiscus mosaic design. I loved it so much I created a coordinating cheese board. Be sure to apply a grout sealer to protect the mosaic surface from food stains.

Sizes:
Cheese board – 12" square
Serving tray – 14-1/2" square

Supplies

Surface:
For the Cheese Board
1/4" plywood, 12" square, edges sanded smooth
4 round wooden knobs, 1-1/2"
Acrylic indoor/outdoor paints – Red, white

For the Serving Tray
Tray with plain bottom and raised sides, 14-1/2" square

Mosaic Supplies:
1 sq. ft. turquoise glass
1 sq. ft. green glass
1/2 sq. ft. lime green glass
1/4 sq. ft. yellow glass
1 sq. ft. red glass
Mosaic glue
Mosaic grout – White
Grout sealer

Tools & Other Supplies:
Basic glass cutting and mosaic tools
Scissors
For the Cheese Board: Paint brush, wood glue

Except for the surface and as noted, use the same supplies and tools for either project.

Instructions for Serving Tray

See the photo sequence "Stained Glass Mosaics" before you begin.

1. Make two copies of the design, using the pattern provided. On one copy, cut out the pieces using regular scissors to make templates.
2. Use the other copy of the pattern to transfer the design to the surface of the tray, using carbon paper.
3. Cut out the pattern pieces, using the templates and your glass cutter.
4. Cut out the background pieces, using the mosaic glass and tile cutters.
5. Glue the pieces to the surface, leaving 1/8" between the pieces for grout. TIP: It's easier to spread glue over a small (3-4") area at a time, then position the glass pieces over the glue instead of trying to apply glue to each small piece. Allow to dry overnight.
6. Apply the grout, wipe, and polish. Allow the grout to dry completely.
7. Apply three to four coats of non-toxic grout sealer. Let dry. ❑

Instructions for Cheese Board

1. Paint all surfaces of the plywood (both sides and all the edges) with white paint. Let dry. Apply as many coats as necessary for complete coverage.
2. Paint the wooden knobs with red paint. Let dry.
3. Using wood glue, attach the four wooden knobs to the bottom of the plywood board.
4. Follow the steps for the Serving Tray, above, to create the mosaic design. ❑

Hawaiian Hibiscus Serving Tray & Cheese Board

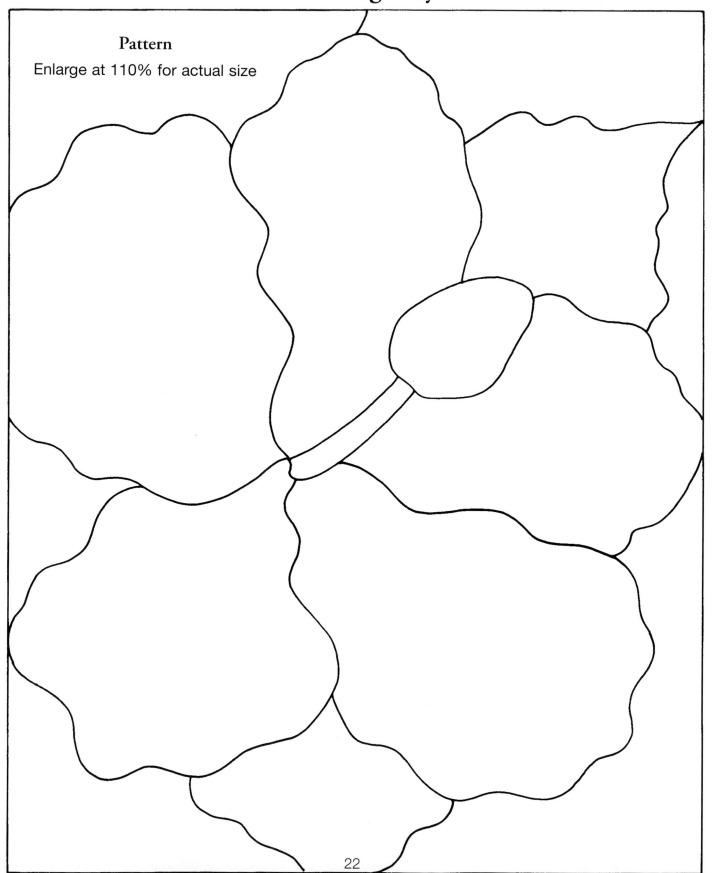

Pattern

Enlarge at 110% for actual size

Fish Bowl Table Top

Pattern

Instructions appear on page 24.

Enlarge at 200% for
actual size

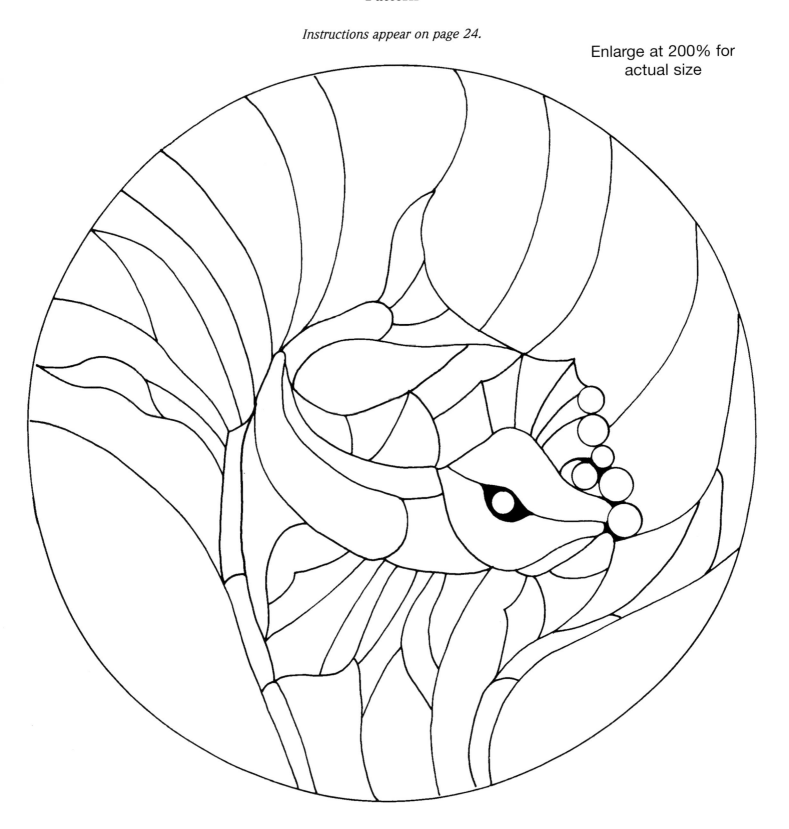

Goldfish Bowl
Table Top

This was the very first mosaic project I did. I didn't really know any other way to create a stained glass design other than to hand cut every piece and then assemble it using glue and grout. I used a round glass disc that I cut to fit a metal table as a base for the mosaic design. It is still my favorite mosaic.
Why not recycle an old table at your house and create your own favorite piece of mosaic art?

Pattern is on page 23.

Size: 15" diameter

Supplies

Surface:
A glass or wood table top,
   15" diameter

Mosaic Supplies:
2 sq. ft. aqua iridized glass
1/2 sq. ft. *each* of 4 or 5 "goldfish colors" of glass (pink, coral, yellow, white)
1 sq. ft. green glass
Clear glass nuggets – 3 medium, 3 small
1 amber glass nugget (for eye)
Mosaic glue
Mosaic grout – Black
Grout sealer

Tools:
Basic tools and supplies (See the section at the beginning of this book.)
Glass grinder

Instructions

See the photo sequence "Stained Glass Mosaics" before you begin.

1. Place your table top over a large piece of pattern paper. Trace around the outside edge to create your pattern template. Adjust the pattern on the previous page to fit your template. Allow 1/2" around the outside edge of the top for grout.

2. Number each pattern piece and make a copy. Using pattern shears, cut out the pattern.

3. Cut out all the glass pieces and shape them to fit the pattern, using a glass grinder.

4. Place the pattern under the table top (if your table top is glass) or transfer the design to the table top (if your table top is wood). *If your table top is glass, coat the surface with a thin layer of glue and let it dry.*

5. Glue the glass pieces to the table top, leaving 1/16" spaces between the glass pieces for the grout and 1/2" around the outside edge of the top for grout. Allow the glue to dry overnight. *(NOTE: A mosaic on a glass surface takes longer to dry than one on a more porous surface.)*

6. Grout the project and allow the grout to dry completely.

7. Apply three to four coats of grout sealer. ❏

Tropical Fish
Tabletop Fountain

Mosaic birdbaths and fountains can be used outside to decorate your garden or indoors to accent a sunroom or back porch. This fountain has four parts: 1) a shallow terra cotta planter (the base) that houses/hides the pump; 2) a terra cotta saucer (the bowl) that sits on top of the shallow planter and is decorated with the fish mosaic; 3) a small terra cotta flower pot (the spout) that is decorated with a mosaic and used upside down; 4) a glazed tall flower pot used as a stand for the fountain. This last pot can be eliminated if you choose to place your fountain on a tabletop.

Terra cotta flower pots and saucers of various sizes are easy to find and provide an unlimited array of design possibilities. The flower pot or container that you select for the base of your fountain must be large enough to hold three-and-a-half pints of water and deep enough to allow the pump to be completely submerged. To house the pump and water, I used a two-and-a-half quart plastic paint bucket to hold the pump and trimmed off the top edge so the plastic container was the same height as the top of the base. (See Photo 2.) If you don't use this, the terra cotta base will absorb water and may start leaking water out. It's a good idea to purchase the pump first and then select the sizes of flower pots for your project. Small submersible water pumps are available at garden shops and pet stores.

Supplies

Surface:
Fountain Base – 1 shallow terra cotta flower pot, 4" deep (or a size that will accommodate the height of your pump)
Fountain Bowl – 1 deep terra cotta saucer, 14" diameter
Fountain spout – 1 small flower pot, 4"
Stand for your fountain (optional)

Mosaic Supplies:
1 sq. ft. light blue glass
1/4 sq. ft. *each* red, yellow, green, aqua, black, lime, blue, and pink glass
1/2 sq. ft. *each* dark blue, white glass
1 lb. terra cotta grout
Mosaic glue
Grout sealer

Other Supplies:
1 plastic container, 4" x 6" (to use as a water reservoir for the pump, placed inside the base)
1 submersible pump
10" plastic tubing to fit pump
Florist's putty

Tools:
Basic tools and supplies (See the section at the beginning of this book.)
Power drill with masonry drill bits
Masonry file
Craft knife (for trimming the plastic container)
Black permanent marker

Instructions on page 28

Constructing Fountain

Photo 1. Making a notch in the side of the flower pot that is the base of the fountain.

Photo 2. Positioning the pump and the power supply cord in the plastic container in the base.

Photo 3. Assembling the fountain, threading the tubing through the hole in the saucer and the hole in the spout flower pot.

Instructions

See the photo sequence "Stained Glass Mosaics" before you begin.

Prepare the Base, Flower Pot & Saucer:

1. Be sure the diameter of the hole in the bottom of the flower pot you're using as the spout is large enough to accommodate the tubing. If it's not, use a masonry drill or file to enlarge it.

2. Drill a 1" diameter hole in the center of the bottom of the saucer. (You need enough space for the pump tubing plus some extra space so the water can drain back into the water reservoir (the plastic container inside the base) that contains the submersible pump.)

3. File a 1" notch in the top rim of the base flower pot to accommodate the pump cord. (Photo 1) You may need to notch the edge of the plastic container as well. Use a utility knife for this. (See Photo 2.)

Cut the Glass:

1. Using carbon paper and the patterns provided, transfer the designs to the surface of the saucer and spout flower pot. Outline the design with a permanent black felt tip marker for better visibility.

2. Hand cut the pattern pieces with a glass cutter. Use grozing pliers or a glass grinder to shape the pieces.

3. Use the glass and tile cutters to cut the background pieces.

Glue & Grout:

1. Coat the outside surface of the spout flower pot and the inside bottom surface of the saucer with a thin coat of mosaic glue. Let dry for a few minutes.

2. Apply more glue and position the hand cut mosaic pieces, following the pattern lines for placement. Leave 1/2" of space around the outside edges and 1/8" space between the glass pieces.

3. Fill the spaces around the pattern pieces on the bottom of the saucer and on the sides and bottom of the outside of the spout flower pot with the background glass pieces. Let dry for 24 hours.

4. Use terra cotta mosaic grout to fill the spaces between the pieces. Clean up and let dry 48 hours.

5. Seal and protect the fountain with three coats of grout sealer. Allow to dry completely.

Assemble the Fountain:

NOTE: It is very important that all parts of the fountain are completely dry during assembly.

1. Place the plastic container in the base pot. Use florist's putty to secure the plastic container to the bottom of the base pot.

2. Place the pump in the plastic bucket with the tubing coming out the top and the cord coming out the side and through the notch in the side of the base. (Photo 2)

3. Fill the plastic container with water. Feed the pump tubing up through the bottom of the saucer and place the saucer over the base. Place the small flower pot (the spout) in the center of the saucer with the end of the tubing threaded through the hole in the bottom of the pot. (Photo 3)

4. Place the fountain on a table or stand. Plug in the fountain. ❏

Pattern for Lotus on Spout

Actual size

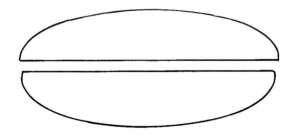

Patterns for Fish

Actual size

Avian Spa
Birdbath

Most times, less is more. I found this great cobalt blue glazed birdbath at my local garden center – it was love at first sight. The price was $35, and I was out the door. I placed it in my backyard and stared at that pretty treasure for weeks before I decided to add simple, elegant rings of mirrored art glass around the base. The black grout simply disappears. Displaying pieces of sea glass and small shells in the bowl adds interest.

Supplies

Surface:
Medium-size ceramic birdbath

Mosaic Supplies:
2 sq. ft. *each* gold, blue, and green
   mirrored art glass
Mosaic glue
Mosaic grout – Black
Grout sealer

Tools & Other Supplies:
Paper plates
Basic tools and supplies (See the section at the beginning of this book.)

Design Tips

- Garage sales, flea markets, and antique shops are great places to find interesting surfaces for garden mosaics.
- When you use cement and terra cotta containers, make sure they are clean, not cracked, and free of grease.
- Be kind to birds and other wildlife! If you create a mosaic inside the bowl of a birdbath or fountain, seal with a non-toxic sealer.

Instructions

See the photo sequence "Stained Glass Mosaics" before you begin.

1. Use your glass cutter and a ruler to cut 1" and 3/4" strips of glass. Cut the strips into 1" sections. Place the pieces on paper plates, separating them by color.
2. Brush a coat of glue over the entire surface where you plan to place the glass pieces. Let it dry a few minutes. TIP: When working on a rounded vertical surface, coating the entire area with glue gives the pieces something to grab hold of – they are less likely to slide off.
3. Working one small area at a time, glue the glass pieces to the base. Don't leave any additional space for grout. The curve of the round columnar base will create the grout spaces. TIP: It's easier to spread glue over one small (3-4") area of the surface at a time and then position the glass pieces on the surface rather than brushing glue on each small piece and pressing it in place.
4. When all the pieces are in place, allow the glue to dry overnight. TIP: To keep larger pieces of glass from sliding, try using a little masking tape to hold them in place until the glue sets up.
5. Grout the project and allow the grout to dry completely.
6. Apply three to four coats of grout sealer. ❑

It's a Party
Table Top

Here's a wonderful birthday present – one the recipient can use year after year.
The great thing about this project is you can use it for anyone's birthday. Around our house,
it's not a real birthday celebration without this family favorite decked out with
balloons, cupcakes, flowers, and lots of good wishes.
This table top can be used on any table base. When the party is over, just slip it inside a
cardboard sleeve and roll it into the storage closet until the next birthday party.

Size: 24" diameter

Supplies

Surface:
Round clear glass table top, 1/4"
    thick, 24" diameter

Mosaic Supplies:
3 sq. ft. white glass
1 china dessert plate
1 sq. ft. pink glass
1/2 sq. ft. *each* purple, yellow, and
    green glass
6 large blue glass nuggets or jewels
Mosaic glue
Mosaic grout white

Tools & Other Supplies:
Basic tools and supplies (See the sec-
    tion at the beginning of this book.)
Paper plates

Design Tips

- You can enlarge this project to any
  size you wish – think about creating a setting for four on your
  glass-topped patio table.
- If you make a bigger table top, use
  a different colored or patterned
  plate for each place setting to really jazz it up. Save broken plates or
  buy pretty ones inexpensively at
  yard sales or thrift stores.

Instructions

See the photo sequence "Stained Glass Mosaics" before you begin.

Prepare:

1. Place the glass table top over a large piece of pattern paper. Trace around the outside edge to create your pattern template.

2. Position the china plate on the template and trace around the outside edge.

3. Use tracing paper to transfer the balloon, hat, and other design elements to the
   pattern template, using the photo as a guide for placement.

Cut & Glue:

1. Cut the glass into random shapes – even the glass nuggets – using mosaic glass
   and tile cutters. Place the pieces, sorted by color, on separate paper plates.

2. Place the pattern under the glass table top.

3. Working a few pieces at a time, use the mosaic cutters to nip the china plate into
   pieces and glue the pieces to the glass table top. (Working a few pieces at a time
   will allow you to re-assemble the plate pieces in order on the table top.) Leave
   1/8" between the pieces for grout.

4. Glue the glass pieces for the design elements, using the mosaic cutters as needed
   for fitting. Don't forget to leave 1/8" spaces between the glass pieces for grout.

5. Glue down the background pieces. Be sure to allow 1/4" of space around the
   outside edge of the glass top for grout. Let dry overnight. TIP: Spread glue over
   one small (3-4") area at a time and position the glass pieces on the glue-covered
   surface rather than trying to brush glue on each small piece.

Grout & Seal:

1. Mix and apply the grout. Allow the grout to dry completely.

2. Apply three to four coats of grout sealer. The sealer is very important, especially
   for table tops – it protects them from the weather and from food and beverage
   stains. ❑

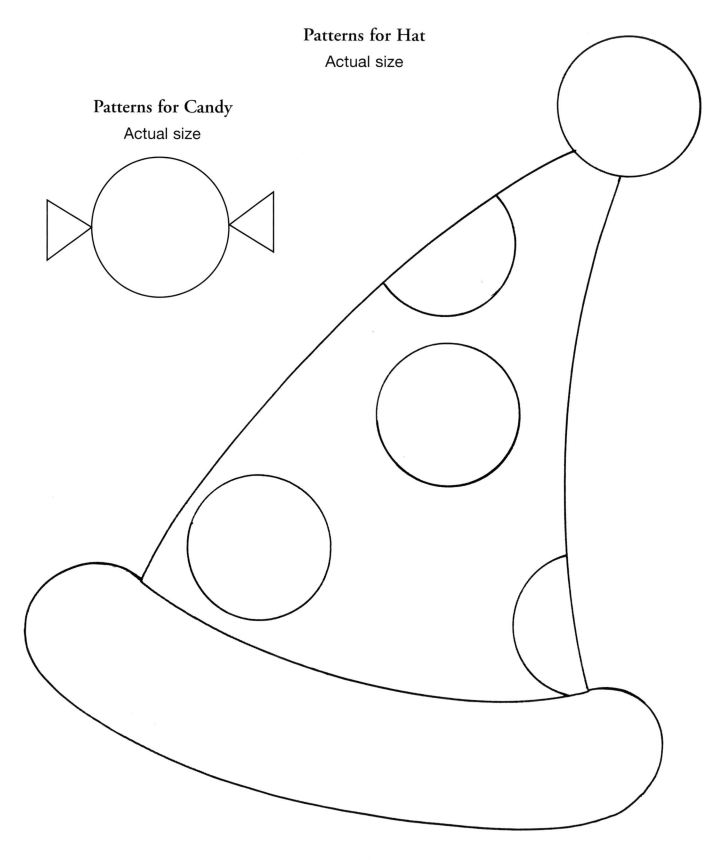

Patterns for Hat

Actual size

Patterns for Candy

Actual size

Pattern for Streamers

Actual size

**Pattern for
Happy Birthday**

Actual size

**Pattern for
Balloon End**

Actual size

Use a compass
or dinner plate to
draw a 9" – 10"
circle for balloon.

Tea for Two
Table Top

This is the perfect table for a tea party. The mosaic table top features a real china plate and silverware created out of mirror glass. The stained glass napkin will never have to be laundered, and the pink roses never need watering. You can hand cut the roses and silverware with a glass cutter or assemble them from random-shaped pieces of glass you cut with mosaic cutters. This mosaic can be enlarged to any size you wish. On larger table tops, you could add additional place settings.

Size: 24" diameter

Supplies

Surface:
Round clear glass table top, 1/4" thick, 24" diameter

Mosaic Supplies:
3 sq. ft. yellow/white glass
1 china dinner plate
1 sq. ft. silver mirror glass
1/4 sq. ft. *each* blue, green and pink glass
Mosaic glue
Mosaic grout white
Grout sealer

Tools & Other Supplies:
Basic tools and supplies (See the section at the beginning of this book.)
Paper plates

Instructions

See the photo sequence "Stained Glass Mosaics" before you begin.

Prepare:
1. Place your glass table top over a large piece of pattern paper. Trace around the outside edge to create a pattern template.
2. Position the china plate on the template and trace around the outside edge.
3. Using tracing paper, transfer the rose design, silverware, and napkin to the pattern paper.
4. *Option:* If you are going to hand cut the roses and the silverware, make an additional copy of these designs and cut out the pieces, using pattern shears.

Cut & Glue:
1. Cut the pieces for the roses and silverware, either hand cutting the pieces with a glass cutter using the templates you made or cutting random shapes with mosaic cutters. Place the pieces, sorted by color, on separate paper plates.
2. Cut the random-shaped pieces for the background and napkin using mosaic cutters. Place the pieces, sorted by color, on separate paper plates.
3. Place the pattern under the glass table top.
4. Working a few pieces at a time, use the mosaic cutters to nip the china plate into pieces and glue the pieces to the glass table top. (Working a few pieces at a time will allow you to re-assemble the plate pieces in order on the table top.) Leave 1/8" between the pieces for grout.
5. Glue the glass pieces for the roses and silverware, using the mosaic cutters as needed for fitting. Don't forget to leave 1/8" spaces between the glass pieces for grout. If you're using random pieces, spread glue over one small (3-4") area at a time and position the glass pieces on the glue-covered surface rather than trying to brush glue on each small piece.
6. Glue the pieces for the napkin in place, again leaving 1/8" between the pieces for grout.
7. Glue the background pieces, spreading the glue over one small area at a time and placing the pieces on the surface. Allow 1/4" around the outside edge of the glass top for grout. When all the pieces are in place, allow the glue to dry overnight.

Grout & Seal:
1. Grout the project. Allow the grout to dry completely.
2. Apply three to four coats of grout sealer to protect the table top from the weather and from food and beverage stains. ❏

Napkin Pattern

Actual size

Flatware Patterns

Actual size

Rose Pattern

Actual size

Red, White & Blue
Patio Accessories

My granddaughter and I made these one July afternoon, recycling an old flower pot and a glass votive. Mosaic flower pots are fun and easy because they are generally free-form designs – you don't need a pattern.
Look around – I'm sure you can find lots of simple surfaces that could be transformed by mosaics into celebratory seasonal decorations. Keep the design simple, and use small pieces. This advice works for any color scheme. If fall is more your season, use yellows, golds, reds, and rich greens.

Supplies

Surfaces:
Terra cotta flower pot, 5"
Glass votive, 2"

Mosaic Supplies:
Scraps of red, white, and blue glass
Mosaic glue
Mosaic grout – White
Grout sealer

Tools & Other Supplies:
Basic tools and supplies (See the section at the beginning of this book.)
Masking tape
Tracing paper
Pencil
Scissors

Crafting with Children

Doing arts and crafts is a great way to spend time with your children and grandchildren. (It's a fact that all children do better when they participate in arts and crafts.) The act of creating art bridges all gaps, unleashing the memory and creating memories.

Instructions for Flower Pot

See the photo sequence "Stained Glass Mosaics" before you begin.

Prepare & Cut:

1. *If you want to sketch out your idea,* use a pencil and draw directly on the flower pot. *If you want to create a free-form design,* lay out the pieces on your work surface after cutting them. Re-arrange them until you find a design that pleases you.

2. Cut the glass into random shapes, using mosaic glass cutters – even the glass nuggets. Start by cutting simple shapes.

Photo 1. Masking off the area of the pot not covered by the mosaic.

Glue:

1. Brush a coat of glue on the entire area where the mosaic is to be placed. Let it dry a few minutes. (This gives the glass pieces something to grab hold of – they're less likely to slide.)

2. Glue the pieces to the flower pot. Leave 1/8" between the pieces and at least 1/2" of space around the outside edges of the mosaic area for

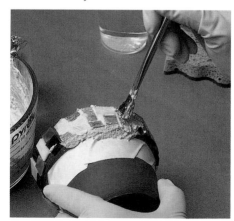
Photo 2. Brushing grout over the mosaic area.

grout. TIP: Spread glue over a small (2-3") area at a time, then position the glass pieces on the glue-covered surface. This is easier than brushing glue on each small piece before sticking it on the pot.

3. When all the pieces are in place, allow the glue to dry one to two hours. TIP: To keep larger pieces of glass from slipping, use a little masking tape to hold them in place until the glue sets up. Remove the tape before grouting.

Grout & Seal:

1. If only part of the surface is to be grouted, mask off the other areas with tape. (Photo 1)

2. Apply the grout with a brush over the mosaic area (Photo 2). When all of the mosaic is grouted (Photo 3), allow to dry completely.

3. Apply a coat of grout sealer. (Sealer will protect the pot from the weather and from salt and plant stains.) ❏

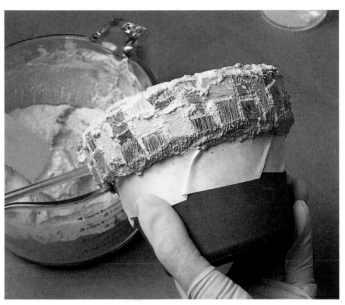

Photo 3. Grout is applied and the mosaic is ready to wipe.

Instructions for Candle Holder

See the photo sequence "Stained Glass Mosaics" before you begin.

Prepare & Cut:

1. Draw a star motif to fit your candle holder. Trace the star motif on a piece of paper. Cut the paper pattern to fit inside your candle holder.

2. Cut the glass into random shapes, using mosaic glass cutters – even the glass nuggets. Start by cutting simple shapes.

Glue:

1. Brush a coat of glue over the surface of the votive. Let it dry a few minutes. (This gives the glass pieces something to grab hold of – they're less likely to slide.)

2. Slip the paper pattern inside the candle holder and, using the pattern as a guide, glue the pieces to the candle holder. Leave 1/8" between the pieces and at least 1/2" of space around the outside edges of the mosaic for grout. Use tweezers to help position small pieces of glass. TIP: Spread glue over a small (2-3") area at a time, then position the glass pieces on the glue-covered surface. This is easier than brushing glue on each small piece before sticking it on the pot.

3. When all the pieces are in place, allow the glue to dry one to two hours. TIP: To keep larger pieces of glass from slipping, use a little masking tape to hold them in place until the glue sets up. Remove the tape before grouting.

Grout & Seal:

1. Apply the grout with a brush over the mosaic. When working with small round objects such as this candle holder, it is helpful to place the item over a bottle of paint or a small plastic jar. (Photo 4) Allow the grout to dry completely.

2. Apply a coat of grout sealer. ❏

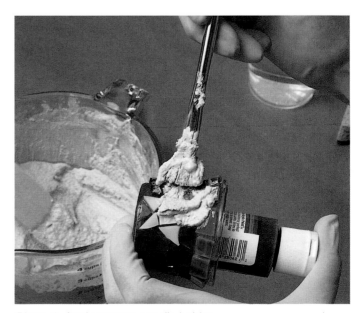

Photo 4. Apply grout to candle holder.

Roses are Red, Bees are Yellow
Patio Table

I am always on the lookout for small wooden tables that I can decorate and set out at parties. I found this unfinished table at my local crafts store. It's the perfect size and provided a great surface for mosaics. This table is so cute it would be a shame to put it away after the party.
You can use pre-cut glass motifs or cut your own, using the pattern provided.
A table top covered with a glass mosaic is extremely durable if you use a good grout sealer to protect the surface from stains.

Table size: 19" x 22"

Supplies

Surface:
Wooden table

Mosaic Supplies:
2 pre-cut glass bumblebees
1 pre-cut glass rose
2 sq. ft. light blue glass
1/4 sq. ft. black glass
1/2 sq. ft. cream glass
If you decide to cut your own bumblebees and rose, you will need to purchase additional black, red, deep red, green, yellow, and white iridized glass.
Mosaic glue
Mosaic grout – Light gray
Grout sealer

Tools & Other Supplies:
Lime green acrylic paint
Varnish
Basic tools and supplies (See the section at the beginning of this book.)
Painting supplies – Sandpaper, tack cloth, paint brush

Instructions

See the photo sequence "Stained Glass Mosaics" before you begin.

Paint the Table:
1. Sand the table and wipe away the sanding dust.
2. Paint the table with two coats of lime green acrylic paint. Let dry completely.
3. Apply varnish to all areas of the table except the shelf and the top.

Cut the Glass:
If you're using pre-cut glass motifs, skip steps 1, 2, and 3.
1. Trace the patterns and number all the pieces.
2. Using carbon paper, transfer the designs to the table.
3. Cut out all the glass pieces for the bumblebees and rose, using the pattern templates.
4. Use mosaic glass cutters to cut the background pieces.

Glue the Mosaic to the Table Top & Grout:
1. Using mosaic glue, adhere all the rose pieces and one bumblebee to the table top. Use the photo as a guide for placement. Leave 1/16" between the glass pieces for grout.
2. Glue the background pieces around the motifs, using the mosaic cutters to make additional cuts as needed. Leave 1/2" around the outside edge and 1/16" between the glass pieces for grout. TIP: It's easier to spread glue over one small (3-4") area at a time and then position the glass pieces on the glue-covered surface instead of brushing glue on each small piece. When all the mosaic pieces are in place, allow the glue to dry overnight.
3. Grout the project the next day with gray grout. (If you can't find gray grout, see "Coloring Grout" on page 58.) Allow the grout to dry completely.

Seal & Add the Second Bee:
1. Apply three to four coats of grout sealer to protect the tabletop from the weather and from stains.
2. If you table has a shelf, decorate it by simply gluing the second bee and a trail of black glass dashes as a flight line. (You can cut these with mosaic cutters.) **Don't** grout this design. ❏

Pattern for Rose

Actual size

Pattern for Bee
Actual size

Mixed Blues
Flower Pots & Birdhouse
The birdhouse is pictured on page 51.

I love creating designs in different mediums. These two flower pots and the birdhouse are decorated with the remains of two blue willow pattern china plates that found their way to the floor during a crowded dinner party. Instead of crying over spilt milk or, in this case, broken plates, I decided to recycle them – along with some scrap art glass – and decorate two flower pots and a birdhouse. Now when I host an outdoor cookout, I set the table with my good (unbroken) plates and decorate the table with these coordinated flower pots. The birdhouse has become a swanky condo for the birds in my backyard.

Supplies

Surfaces:
2 terra cotta flower pots, 5"
Wooden birdhouse, 10" tall

Mosaic Supplies:
2 blue-and-white dinner plates
1 sq. ft. yellow art glass
20 (approx.) dark blue glass nuggets
Scraps of green art glass
4 blue buttons
Mosaic glue
Mosaic grout – White
Non-toxic grout sealer

Tools & Other Supplies:
Basic tools and supplies (See the section at the beginning of this book.)
Pencil
Masking tape

Continued on page 50

Instructions for Random-Pattern Flower Pot

This flower pot is a free-form design – you don't need a pattern. See the photo sequence "Stained Glass Mosaics" before you begin.

1. Cut one plate into random shapes, using mosaic glass cutters. **Don't** try and break the plate with a hammer – it will smash the material and you won't have good random-shaped pieces.
2. Brush a coat of glue over the outside of the flower pot. Let it dry a few minutes. (This is a good technique to use when you're covering a rounded, vertical surface with a mosaic – it gives the pieces something to grab hold of, and the pieces are less likely to slide.)
3. Glue the pieces to the flower pot. Leave 1/8" between the pieces and at least 1/2" of space around the top and bottom edges for grout. TIP: Spread glue over one small (3-4") area at a time, then position the pieces on the glue-covered area instead of brushing glue on each small piece and pressing it on the pot.
4. When all the pieces are in place, allow the glue to dry four hours or overnight. TIP: Use a little masking tape to secure larger pieces in place until the glue sets up. Remove the tape before grouting.
5. Grout the flower pot. Allow the grout to dry completely.
6. Apply three to four coats of grout sealer to protect the pot from the weather and from salt and plant stains. ❏

Instructions for Daisy Flower Pot

See the photo sequence "Stained Glass Mosaics" before you begin.

1. Using a pencil, sketch the placement of the four daisies on the sides of the pot.
2. Cut out the daisy petals from plate fragments, using the mosaic glass cutters.
3. Cut the stems and leaves from green glass scraps, using the mosaic glass cutters.
4. Cut the yellow glass for the background into random shapes, using the mosaic glass cutters.
5. Brush a coat of glue over the outside of the flower pot. Let it dry a few minutes.
6. Glue a button at the center of each daisy.
7. Working one daisy at a time, spread glue over the petal area, then position the petal pieces on the glue-covered area. (This is easier than brushing glue on each small piece and pressing it on the pot.)
8. Working one side of the pot at a time, use the same technique to glue the stems and leaves in place.
9. Glue the yellow glass background pieces to the flower pot around the daisies. Leave 1/8" between the pieces and at least 1/2" of space around the bottom edge for grout. TIP: Spread glue over one small area at a time, then position the pieces over the glue.
10. Glue the glass nuggets around the rim of the flower pot. Allow the glue to dry overnight.
11. Grout the flower pot. Allow the grout to dry completely.
12. Apply three to four coats of grout sealer to protect the pot from the weather and from salt and plant stains. ❏

Instructions for Birdhouse

This birdhouse is a free-form design – you don't need a pattern. See the photo sequence "Stained Glass Mosaics" before you begin.

1. Cut a plate into random-shaped pieces, using mosaic glass cutters. **Don't** try to break the plate with a hammer – it will smash the material and you won't have good random-shaped pieces.
2. Glue the pieces to the birdhouse. Leave 1/8" between the pieces and at least 1/2" of space around each edge for grout. TIP: Spread glue over one small (3-4") area at a time, then position the pieces on the glue-covered area instead of brushing glue on each small piece and pressing it in place.
3. When all the pieces are in place, allow the glue to dry four hours or overnight. TIP: Use a little masking tape to secure larger pieces in place until the glue sets up. Remove the tape before grouting.
4. Grout the birdhouse, covering the edges of the roof and corners with grout. Allow the grout to dry completely.
5. Apply three to four coats of grout sealer to protect the birdhouse from the weather. For the birds' sake, be sure to select a non-toxic sealer. ❏

Design Tip

Garage sales, flea markets, thrift stores, and antique shops are great places to find interesting plates for mosaics. Look for ones that have a busy pattern and lots of color. Coordinate them with solid colored art glass. Plates with chipped rims or small cracks work great for mosaics and are easy on your budget.

Paris Flea Market
Table Top

Black and white is my favorite color combination. The contrast of rich black and crisp white never fails to receive rave reviews. I recycled a 1950s metal garden table for this project. The table's original glass top broke years ago so I cut a new wooden top and decorated it with this Paris-inspired mosaic. The black-and-white harlequin design is accented with a random-cut black border with bands of pure yellow.

You can adapt the concept and design to **any size of table top**. Rather than providing exact measurements for the top I created, I have included instructions for creating diamond shapes for any size table top you wish. Your goal is a diamond design with all the diamonds the same size and with half-diamonds on the edges. My table top has five rows of black diamonds with three black diamonds in each row. The black diamonds alternate with white diamonds. Since making this tabletop I have devised a much **easier way** to create a pattern that will give you four rows of whole diamonds (instead of five).

Supplies

Surface:
Black metal table base
Pressure treated plywood, 1/2" thick, cut
   to fit the table top

Mosaic Supplies:
Black, white, and yellow glass (Measure
   your table top to estimate how much
   you'll need.)
Mosaic glue
Mosaic grout – White
Grout sealer

Tools & Other Supplies:
White acrylic paint
Colored chalk
Measuring tape
General mosaic and glass cutting tools
General pattern supplies and tools
Optional: Strip cutter

Instructions

Paint the Table Top:
Paint the plywood with two coats of white paint. Let dry completely. Be sure to paint all the edges and both sides.

Lay Out the Design:
1. Cut a piece of pattern paper to fit your table top. Piece it with tape, if necessary.
2. Draw a 1/2" border around the outside edge of the paper pattern. (This marks the edge of the mosaic – the area outside this line is for the grout on the edge.)
3. For the outer yellow band, measure and mark a 1/2" band inside the grout line.
4. For the black border, decide the width you would like it to be so that it is in proportion to the table top. A larger top would require a wider border than a smaller top. For most tables, a border of 1"-3" would be appropriate.
5. For the inner yellow band, draw a 1/2" border inside the black border.
6. Your diamond design will fit into the remainder of the space. Measure this space to find the center of the pattern. Divide the space into quarters lengthwise, then divide the space into quarters widthwise. You now have 16 sections.
7. Draw lines diagonally from corner to corner within each 16th section, creating Xs across every space. This will give you the diamond pattern. Decide which diamonds will be black and which ones will be white and color the black ones in.
8. Transfer this pattern to the painted wooden table top, using colored chalk.

Cut & Glue:
See the photo sequence "Stained Glass Mosaics" before you begin.
1. Make a template for cutting the diamonds by tracing a diamond shape on pattern paper. Trim off 1/32" on all sides to allow 1/16" for the grout between each mosaic piece.
2. Cut out all the glass pieces for the black diamonds, the white diamonds, and yellow bands, using a strip cutter or hand cutter.
3. Use mosaic cutters to cut the random black shapes.
4. Using mosaic glue, adhere all the diamond pieces to the board, spacing the pieces 1/16" apart to allow space for the grout between the pieces.
5. Glue the pieces of the yellow bands in place.
6. Glue down the black random shaped pieces between the two yellow bands. (It's easier to spread glue over a small (3-4") area and position the glass pieces on the glue-covered surface instead of brushing glue on each small piece and pressing it on the surface.) When all the pieces are in place, allow the glue to dry overnight.

Grout & Seal:
1. Grout the project. Allow the grout to dry completely.
2. Apply three to four coats of recommended grout sealer. (The sealer is very important, especially for table tops. It protects them from the weather and from stains.)

Iridescent Glow
Vase or Candle Holder

Have you seen the art glass that changes colors as the light hits the surface? There's a name for this glass – dichroic. It is expensive, but worth it, in my opinion. Its iridized shine and ability to change colors with the light make it highly desirable for jewelry and mosaics. I used clear and pink dichroic glass for this two-in-one project. This vase can be used as a candle holder as well. The light from the candle creates a beautiful glow seen through this translucent glass.

Size: 14" tall

Supplies

Base:
Clear glass vase, 14" tall

Glass:
1 sq. ft. clear dichroic glass
1/4 sq. ft. pink dichroic glass
Mosaic glue
Mosaic grout
Grout sealer

Tools & Other Supplies:
Basic tools and supplies (See the section at the beginning of this book.)
Paper plates

Instructions

See the photo sequence "Stained Glass Mosaics" before you begin.

Cut:
1. Cut triangular shaped pieces of pink glass for the flower petals. (These are free-form flowers; you don't need a pattern.)
2. Cut 1/2" circles of pink glass for the flower centers and for accents.
3. Cut random-shaped pieces of clear glass for the background.
4. Place the pieces on separate paper plates.

Glue:
1. Brush a coat of glue on the entire surface of the vase and let dry a few minutes. (This is especially helpful when working on rounded surfaces.)

2. Glue the round pink pieces for the flower centers, using the photo as a guide for placement. Glue the flower petals around the flower centers. Scatter the pink circles and flowers over the surface.
3. Glue the background pieces, placing them around the flowers and round accents. TIP: Work one area at a time, spreading glue over a 3-4" area and positioning the glass pieces on the glue-covered surface. It's easier than brushing glue on each small piece. When all the pieces are in place, allow the glue to dry overnight. Glass-on-glass mosaics take longer to dry than mosaics on more porous surfaces like wood.

Grout:
1. Grout the project. Allow to dry completely.
2. Apply three to four coats of grout sealer. Let dry. ❑

Summer Nights
Candle Lantern

I love to turn the ordinary into extraordinary. I purchased a plain glass lantern at my home store for $10. I added iridized turquoise glass squares, crystal beads, and a fused glass medallion. Voila! I had an original work of art. Go ahead – light up your trees with hanging lanterns!

Size: 10" tall, 5" diameter

Supplies

Base:
Glass lantern with wire hanger

Mosaic Supplies:
1 sq. ft. turquoise glass
Mosaic glue
Mosaic grout
Crystals
Fused glass accent piece
Jewelry wire
Grout sealer

Tools:
Basic tools and supplies (See the section at the beginning of this book.)
Jewelry pliers

Design Tips

- You can fuse your own glass pieces or find some great ones at crafts stores. Or recycle a pendant or a brooch to decorate your creation.
- Drape a string of pearls or beads around the neck of this project for another marvelous look.

Instructions

See the photo sequence "Stained Glass Mosaics" before you begin.

1. Remove the glass lantern from the holder.
2. Cut the glass into 1/2" squares.
3. Brush a coat of glue on the entire surface. Let it dry a few minutes. (This provides a sticky surface and helps eliminate sliding.)
4. Starting at the bottom edge of the lantern, glue the squares in a spiral formation. Once you have placed the first spiral, continue gluing pieces in rows along the spiral. Cover the entire glass surface, leaving 1/16" between the pieces and the rows. When all the pieces are in place, allow the glue to dry overnight. Glass-on-glass mosaics take longer to dry than mosaics on more porous surfaces.
5. Grout the project. Allow the grout to dry completely.
6. Apply three to four coats of grout sealer. Let dry.
7. Place the lantern back in the holder.
8. Make a necklace for your lantern by stringing the crystal beads and the fused glass medallion on the jewelry wire. Place the necklace round the neck of the lantern. Twist the ends of the wire together. Trim off the excess wire. ❑

The Green Man

Garden Plaque

Designed by Denny Berkery

The Green Man is the protector of the woods, so he's the perfect addition to anyone's garden wall. This project was very easy to create. I used a piece of pressure-treated plywood for the base, attached the cement Green Man plaque, and surrounded it with glass nuggets for grapes and glass mosaic leaves. Cement plaques are available at stained glass stores and garden centers and on-line. You could substitute a decorative ceramic tile for the plaque.

Panel size: 12" square

Supplies

Surface:
Pressure-treated plywood, 12" square
Decorative plaque, 5-1/2" x 6-7/8"
40 (approx.) medium-size purple nuggets
1 sq. ft. *each* aqua and green glass
Construction adhesive (the kind that comes in a tube like caulk – you can buy it at hardware and building supply stores)
Mosaic glue
Mosaic grout – Light gray
Grout sealer

Other Supplies & Tools:
Metal picture hanger
Gray acrylic paint
Basic tools and supplies (See the section at the beginning of this book.)

Instructions

See the photo sequence "Stained Glass Mosaics" before you begin.

Prepare:

1. Paint the wood with two coats of gray acrylic paint. Let dry completely. Be sure to paint all edges and both sides.

2. Attach the metal picture hanger to the back of the board. (It's important to do this **before** you start the mosaic.)

3. Trace the pattern, number all the pieces, and make a copy. Use pattern shears to cut out one copy to make the pattern templates.

4. Using carbon paper, transfer the design to the front of the plywood.

Cut:

1. Cut out all the leaf and vine pieces from green glass, using the templates.

2. For the background, hand cut 1/2" square glass tiles from aqua glass.

Glue:

1. Glue the plaque to the center of the board using construction adhesive. Let dry according to the directions on the label.

2. Use mosaic glue to adhere all the leaves and vines according to the pattern. Don't forget to leave 1/2" around the outside edge and 1/16" between the glass pieces for grout.

3. Glue the nuggets in place.

4. Glue the aqua background pieces in place. TIP: Spread glue over one small (3-4") area at a time and then position the glass pieces on the glue-covered surface – it's easier than brushing glue on the pieces one at a time. When all the pieces are in place, allow the glue to dry overnight.

Grout & Seal:

1. Grout the project. (If you can't find gray grout, see "Coloring Grout.") Allow the grout to dry completely.

2. Apply three to four coats of grout sealer to protect the plaque from weather and stains. ❑

Coloring Grout

You may change the color of the grout by adding grout stains (they are sold in tile stores) or by adding colored acrylic paint. If you use grout stain, follow the manufacturer's instructions for mixing. To use paint, replace some of the water with paint when mixing the grout. It's a good idea to select a paint color that is several shades darker than the color you want to achieve — that way, it won't take much paint and the grout will be easier to work with and dry more quickly.

Be sure to mix **all** the grout you need for that project at one time. It is very difficult to achieve exactly the same color mix again (unless you are more organized than I am and carefully measure every ingredient!).

Going to a Garden Party
Cigar Box Purse

Who says you can't take your art with you? This great little cigar box purse makes a lively fashion statement with mosaic dragonflies, a beaded handle, and metallic paint. It is easy to create — and that's a good thing because every woman who sees it is going to ask you to make her one.

Pattern is on page 61

Supplies

Surface:
1 wooden hinged box or cigar box
1 beaded handle
Brass latch

Mosaic Supplies:
1 sq. ft. white art glass
3 pre-cut stained glass dragonflies *or* 1/4. sq. ft. aqua iridized glass (if you're cutting your own)
50 (approx.) white glass nuggets
Mosaic glue
Mosaic grout – White
Grout sealer

Other Supplies & Tools:
Lime green metallic acrylic paint
Clear sealer or varnish
Basic tools and supplies (See the section at the beginning of this book.)
Paint brush
Jewelry pliers (for attaching hardware and handle)
Masking tape
Strong silicone glue

Instructions

Paint the Purse:
1. Remove hinges. Mask off the area of the box where you are going to place the mosaics.
2. Paint the rest of the box – outside and inside – with acrylic paint. Let dry completely. Add a second coat, if needed, for solid coverage and let dry.
3. Seal the paint with clear varnish. Let dry.

Cut & Glue:
1. Use a ruler and a regular glass cutter to cut 1/2" strips of art glass. Cut the strips into 1" pieces. (These will be the background "bricks.") *Option:* Cut small random-shaped glass pieces for the background.
2. *If you're not using pre-cut dragonflies,* cut three dragonflies from aqua glass, using the pattern provided.
3. Glue the nuggets – as close together as possible – to make a border around the outer edges of the mosaic area.
4. Glue the dragonflies in place, leaving enough room between the dragonflies and the nugget border for the background glass pieces. Don't forget to leave a 1/16" space between the pieces for grout.
5. Fill in the background space with the glass "bricks," arranging them like bricks on a wall, staggering each row.

Trim the glass pieces to fit around the dragonflies as you go. TIP: It's easier to spread glue over a small (3-4") area at a time and then position the glass pieces on the glue-covered surface rather than applying glue to each small piece and pressing it in place. When all the pieces are in place, allow the glue to dry four hours or overnight.

Grout & Seal:
1. Grout the project. Let dry completely.
2. Apply three to four coats of grout sealer. (The sealer is very important, especially for projects that are going to be handled a lot.) Let dry.

Finish:
1. Use strong silicone glue to attach four nuggets for "feet" to the bottom edge of the purse. Let dry.
2. Attach all the hardware (handle, latch, etc). ❑

Design Tips

• I used a plain wooden box that I bought at the crafts store, but you could recycle a wooden cigar box – check at your local smoke shop. They generally have a stack of them that they either give away or sell for a couple of dollars.
• I used three pre-cut glass dragonflies to make the mosaic. You could cut your own dragonflies (buy 1/4 sq. ft. aqua iridized glass for this) or use other pre-cut glass motifs.
• Use a coordinating fabric inside the purse instead of paint or paint the inside a different color than the outside.
• Instead of making a purse, decorate the top of a cigar humidor for the Cigar General at your house. He or she would love it!

Pour Your Own Stepping Stones

Creating your own cement stepping stones can be a lot of fun, and they're a terrific way to add a personal touch to your garden. Most of the supplies are available at your local home improvement or hardware store.

Supplies for Stepping Stones

Quick-set cement
A mold *or* form
Art glass
Water
Bucket (for mixing cement)
Trowel (for mixing cement)
Work gloves
Petroleum jelly
A piece of lumber longer than your
    mold is wide (for smoothing)
Self-adhesive paper and permanent
    marker (if you're using the Bottom
    Up Technique – see above)
Grout sealer

About Molds:

You can purchase molds in various sizes and shapes that are designed specifically for casting your own stepping stones, but any object that can hold up to wet cement during the setting process can be used as a mold or form for your stepping stone. I have used pizza boxes, baking pans, and metal trays. You first need to lubricate the mold with petroleum jelly. This acts as a mold release and allows the dry stepping stone to be easily removed from the form.

TIP: Find a place where you can pour your cement in the mold and leave it to dry without having to move it. A garage or carport floor works great. **Don't** set the mold in the sun.

Types of molds – Old baking pans, plastic stepping stone mold, pizza box. (Petroleum jelly is used as a mold release.)

Two Basic Stepping Stone Techniques:

1) **Bottom Up Technique** – Create your design on a piece of self-adhesive paper and place it in the bottom of the mold. Pour wet cement in the mold. (This technique provides more time to work on your design and yields a finer finished project.) The photos and instructions given in this section are for this technique. I think this technique results in a finer finished product.

2) **From the Top Technique** – Pour cement into a stepping stone mold and make sure it is smooth and level. While the cement is still wet, push the decorative elements into the surface of the wet cement.

Iris Stepping Stone

Pattern appears on page 73.

To make this stepping stone, follow the Basic Instructions for the Bottom Up Technique that appear on pages 66 and 67.

Basic Instructions – Bottom Up Technique

1. Create a paper template that fits in the form, leaving a 1" border around the outside edges. Cut this shape out of self-adhesive paper.

2. Transfer your design to the smooth side (not the backing paper or the sticky side) of the self-adhesive paper. (Photo 1)

3. Cut out the glass design or use pre-cut stained glass motifs.

4. Remove the backing paper from the self-adhesive paper. Press the glass pieces, face down, on the sticky side of the paper. (Photo 2)

5. Rub the mold with a generous coat of petroleum jelly.

6. Place the self-adhesive paper with the glass design on it into the bottom of the mold, paper side down. (Photo 3)

7. Mix the cement in a bucket according to the package instructions. TIP: Quick-set cement sets up quickly (you will only have about 15 minutes to pour once the cement is mixed) so have all your materials ready before you start to mix the cement. Mix only as much as you need – you can't save the leftovers for later.

8. Use a trowel to scoop cement from the bucket and place it in the mold over the glass pieces. (Photo 4) Work slowly and carefully so the glass design won't slip or move. Pour or trowel more cement – enough cement to completely fill the mold.

9. Use a piece of wood to level off the top of the stepping stone. (Photo 5) Let it set for a couple of minutes, then gently tap the sides of the mold to release any air bubbles trapped inside the cement. Allow the cement to dry overnight.

10. Remove the stepping stone from the mold. Pull off the plastic self-adhesive paper.

11. If any spaces between the glass pieces did not get filled with cement, mix up a small amount of cement and apply it like mosaic grout to fill in the spaces. Let dry. Allow the stepping stone to cure completely according to the cement manufacturer's instructions.

12. Apply three to four coats of mosaic sealer to all sides of the project. Let dry. Allow to cure one to two weeks before setting the stone outside.

Photo 1 – The pattern is transferred to the self-adhesive paper. The backing paper has been removed.

Photo 2 – The glass pieces are placed, right side down, on the transferred pattern.

Photo 3 – The glass pieces – adhered to the sticky paper – are placed inside the prepared mold.

Photo 4 – Troweling mixed cement into the mold.

Photo 5 – Using a piece of lumber to smooth what will be the bottom of the stepping stone.

Hibiscus Stepping Stone

Use the pattern for the Hawaiian Hibiscus Serving Tray & Cheese Board to cut the glass for this Hibiscus Stepping Stone.

Winter Storage for Stepping Stones & Mosaics

If it freezes during the winter in your area you will want to bring the stepping stones and other mosaic projects indoors. Stack them in your garage or basement during the winter and then return to the yard in the spring. If you are storing flower pots be sure to remove all the dirt from inside the pots. Otherwise, moisture in the dirt will freeze, cracking the pots.

Project Ideas

- You can use pre-cut art glass motifs or create and cut your own design.
- You can also use broken china or pottery, small stones, pieces of terra cotta, or glass nuggets or shapes to make the mosaic.
- Your design can accent the surface or cover the whole stepping stone.
- You can also use this technique to create wall pieces, signs, or house number plaques.
- To use your stepping stone as a plaque, insert a loop of heavy gauge wire or a hanger into the back of the project while the cement is still wet.

Welcome Stepping Stone

Patterns appear on page 74 and 75.

To make this stepping stone, follow the Basic Instructions for the Bottom Up Technique that appear on pages 66 and 67.

Pour Your Own Stepping Stones
Adding Cast Reliefs

Cast cement plaques make attractive, three-dimensional accents for stepping stones when combined with mosaic designs. You can find these plaques at stained glass stores, at garden shops, or on the Internet. To make a stepping stone or plaque with a cast relief, follow the Basic Instructions for the Bottom Up Technique, leaving a blank space in your design for the cast motif.
When you remove the stepping stone from the mold, use construction adhesive to glue the cast plaque to the stepping stone. Finish the edge of the cast piece (and the rest of the top of the stepping stone, if needed) with thin cement or mosaic grout. Clean up the stone with a soft brush and allow to dry completely, then seal.

Sun Stepping Stone

Pattern appears on page 72.

To construct, see information on "Adding Cast Reliefs" and the Basic Instructions for the Bottom Up Technique. The cast sun relief measures 5-3/4" x 6-3/4".

Lady of the Woods Stepping Stone

To construct, see information on "Adding Cast Reliefs" and the Basic Instructions for the Bottom Up Technique.

Lady of the Woods Stepping Stone
Pattern

Enlarge at 165% for actual size

Sun Stepping Stone
Pattern

Enlarge at 200% for actual size

Iris Stepping Stone
Pattern

Actual size

Welcome Stepping Stone
Pattern

Actual size

**Welcome Stepping Stone
Pattern**

Actual size

The Copper Foil Method

Stained glass panels as well as three-dimensional objects like boxes and lampshades can be made using the copper foil method. After the glass pieces are cut and fitted to the pattern, they are wrapped with foil tape and joined together with solder.
The copper foil projects in this section include panels, suncatchers, candle holders, a house number sign, and a garden globe. Each project includes one or more photographs, a list of supplies, and step-by-step instructions. Before you start any project in this section, review the techniques for the copper foil method described and photographed in this section.

Soldering Tools & Supplies

Soldering is the process that holds the foil-wrapped glass pieces together. For soldering, you need the following supplies:

Flux and Brush

Flux is a cleaner that prepares metal to accept the solder. Without flux, soldering isn't possible. I recommend a water-soluble flux, which can be washed off your project with dishwashing soap and water and can be left on your project overnight or until the next day without doing damage.

When you're working, it's a good idea to pour some flux out of the container it comes in and into a wide-mouth jar. Don't ever go back and forth from the container the flux comes in to your project. You'll weaken the strength of the flux if you do.

Apply flux to your project with a **flux brush**. These brushes rust out after a while (continuing exposure to the flux corrodes them), so it's a good idea to buy a couple at a time.

Solder

Solder is the molten metal used to join the metal-wrapped glass pieces in the copper foil technique. It comes on a spool and looks like thick wire. For copper foil, you'll work with a solid-core solder labeled "60/40." The numbers indicate what percentage tin (60%) and lead (40%) are in the solder.

Soldering Iron with Rheostat

To solder stained glass, you need a **soldering iron**, not a soldering gun. You can't use a soldering gun on a stained glass project. The **rheostat** controls the temperature of the soldering iron. Soldering irons come with tips of various sizes. For many copper foil projects, a tip 1/4" wide is used.

An **iron stand** keeps your iron from rolling around on your work surface and protects you from the hot parts of the iron when you are working.

Tip Cleaner

A **tip cleaner** is simply a sponge that is kept wet so that you can wipe off the tip of your soldering iron as you work to keep it clean and completely shiny. If you work with a soldering iron tip that is all dark, you won't be able to do a good job of soldering.

Foiling Supplies

Foil Tape

Foil tape is wrapped around each piece of glass before soldering. One side of the tape is smooth; the other side is sticky. The sticky side goes towards the edge of your glass. Available in copper or silver, foil tape is sold in various widths. The width needed for each project is specified in the individual project instructions.

Foil Burnisher

A **burnisher** is a specialized tool with a roller on one end and a slot on the other. It is used to press the foil tape against the glass and create a tight bond.

You can also burnish foil tape with a wooden chopstick, a craft stick, an orange peeler, or a lathekin.

Pictured clockwise from top left: Foil burnisher, craft knife, copper foil tape, silver foil tape.

Craft Knife

Use a **craft knife** fitted with a #11 blade to cut foil tape.

Assembly Supplies

Glass Squaring Bars

These bars are used along the outer perimeter of a panel to help you square up your project after it is built (provided, of course, that the finished project should be square). You can make your own squaring bars by cutting various lengths of clear glass into 1-1/2" wide strips. You will need bars from 12" to 24" in length. Wrap the edges in **masking tape**. Use **push pins** to hold the squaring bars in place.

Work Table

It is important to select a work table that is at a comfortable height with enough space to accommodate your project when it is completely built plus all the tools and supplies you need to build the project. In your work space, you also want to make sure you have good lighting, convenient access to electrical outlets, good ventilation, and a hard-surface floor that is easy to clean.

Work Boards

Your work board is the surface you'll use for assembling your glass projects. It should fit comfortably on your work table and be at least 2" bigger than the project you're making. A **plywood work board** is best for leading up panels. I like to use 3/8" or 1/2" thick plywood.

You'll need to form a right angle on two sides of your work board for leading up panels. I like to use 1" x 1" stop molding for this. Use a **carpenter's triangle or framing square** and double check the angle you construct (more than once!) to make sure it's perfectly square. If you don't start out square, you will never be able to build a square project!

For copper foil work, an option is to make a work board from **Homasote**, a building material that's often used to make bulletin boards. Buy plywood and Homasote at building supply stores.

If your work space is limited, you can make a portable work board and store it behind a door or in the garage. Don't paint or varnish your work boards.

Miscellaneous Supplies

You'll also need a **desk brush and dust pan** for cleanup and a **cloth rag** for wiping the edges of the glass pieces before you wrap them with foil.

Additional Basic Supplies

*In addition to Soldering Supplies, Foiling Supplies, and Assembly Supplies,
you'll need these supplies for the copper foil method:*

Pattern Making Supplies (See the Basic Tools & Supplies section at the beginning of the book for more information.)

- Pattern fixative or rubber cement
- Pencil and eraser
- Felt-tip pen *or* china marker
- Pattern paper
- 18" metal ruler with cork back
- Transfer paper and tracing paper
- Colored pencils
- Pattern shears

Glass Cutting Tools (See the Basic Tools & Supplies section at the beginning of the book for more information.)

- Carbide glass cutter
- Lubricating oil
- Carborundum stone *or* emery cloth
  Optional: Glass grinder
- Combination Grozing/Breaking Pliers
- Running Pliers

Framing Tools & Supplies

Copper foil panels intended for outdoor use should be wrapped with U-shaped hard metal came made of zinc, brass, or copper. This metal frame provides additional stability and durability.

- Hard metal cames must be cut with a hacksaw or power came saw. If you are going to work with hard metal came, do yourself the favor of investing in a good came saw, a power tool with a circular blade.
- You'll also need a came notcher to cut the hard metal came at a 45-degree angle without cutting the spine of the came. (This makes perfect mitered corners for framing.) If you do not have a notcher, you can cut U-shaped cames with wire cutters.

Safety Gear

- Protective safety glasses
- Face mask

Crafting with Copper Foil

In this section, you'll see how to cut out a pattern, cut glass, use a grinder, put on copper foil, solder, and frame the finished project for display.

Step 1 • Prepare Your Pattern

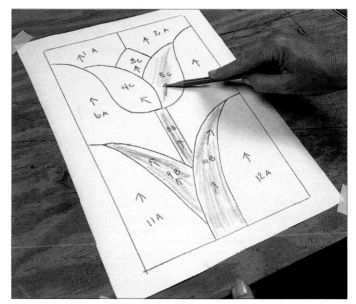

1. Position tracing paper over the pattern and trace the design lines with a pencil. Use arrows to mark the desired direction of the grain of the glass on the pattern. (You want the grain of the glass running in the same direction, no matter the color, so you need to add grain arrows.)

   Once the pattern pieces are cut out, it is often hard to determine the top from the bottom or where they are within a design. It's a good habit to number the pattern pieces so they can be matched with the assembly pattern after cutting. I also add a letter after each number to indicate pattern pieces of a similar color. For example "A" might be the background color; "B" could be the flower color.

2. Transfer the design to white pattern paper or photocopy the traced design. You want to have two copies of the pattern – one to cut apart to make templates for cutting the glass and another to use as a guide when assembling the piece.

3. Color-code the pattern with colored pencils that correspond with glass colors you've chosen. This makes it easier to identify the pattern pieces after you've cut them apart to make the templates.

4. Cut the outside edges of pattern, using a ruler and a craft knife to get a clean, straight edge.

5. Use pattern shears to cut out the pattern pieces you will use as cutting templates. Put the single blade up toward you and start cutting with small strokes, not big ones. Hold your paper in your other hand and cut right along the line. Continue cutting until you have cut out every piece of your pattern. It doesn't matter the order in which you cut it out; do whatever seems easiest for you.

Step 2 • Cut Glass Pieces

Caution! Always wear safety glasses to protect your eyes when cutting glass.

1. Determine how much glass you will need to cut your first piece by positioning the pattern piece on the glass. Divide the larger piece into a smaller, more manageable piece that will be enough to cut all of the pieces of that color. Score that piece of glass from the larger piece, using your glass cutter.

   To break the glass, pick it up and put your fingers under the glass and your thumbs on top. Rock your hands up and away from you. The glass will break along the scored line.

2. Apply pattern fixative or rubber cement to the backs of the pattern pieces. (You could, instead, use spray adhesive or two-sided tape.) Position the pattern pieces on the right (smooth) side of the glass, aligning the arrows you marked on the pattern pieces with the grain of the glass. Allow 1/4"-1/2" all around each piece to make breaking out the pieces easier.

   Option: If you have a light box, you can place the pattern on the light box and position the glass over the pattern. (The pattern lines will be visible through the glass.) Use a china marker or felt-tip marker (one that's not permanent on glass) to transfer the pattern lines to the glass.

3. To begin cutting the first pattern piece, start the cut at the edge of the piece of glass and move the cutter to the edge of the pattern template.

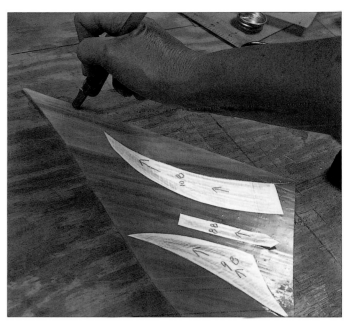

4. Continue the cut along the edge of the pattern template. This photo shows how to hold the cutting tool properly. Note the placement of the fingers and thumb and the angle of the cutting tool in relation to the glass.

5. Finish the cut by continuing past the edge of the pattern template and off the edge of the glass.

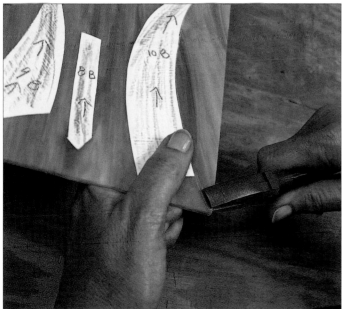

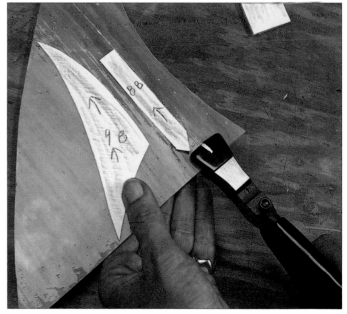

6. Break the glass with breaking pliers or combination pliers, holding the glass surface in one hand and holding the pliers in your other hand. Position the edge of the pliers on the scored line. Use the same technique to score and break the other two sides of the piece – scoring, then breaking; scoring, then breaking. Always score the inside curves first, then the outside curves. Score straight lines last.

7. You can use running pliers on straight cuts. Score the glass from one edge to the other along the pattern template's edge. Align the mark on the running pliers with the scored line to break the glass.

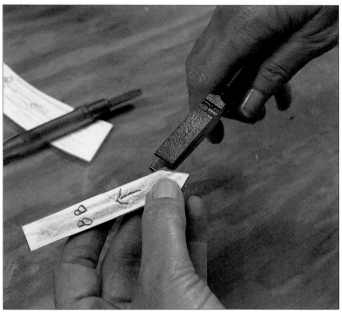

8. Use combination pliers or grozing pliers to break away any small chips or flanges of glass that protrude on the edges of cut pieces. You will save a lot of time if you use your grozing pliers to remove most of the unwanted glass before you go to the carborundum stone, emery cloth, or grinder. **TIP:** To ensure a clean work surface, periodically sweep off your work surface with a brush to remove small chips and slivers of glass that accumulate as you work.

9. To cut deep curves, make successive scores and breaks to gradually move into the final cut. The dotted lines show how this background piece could be scored and separated.

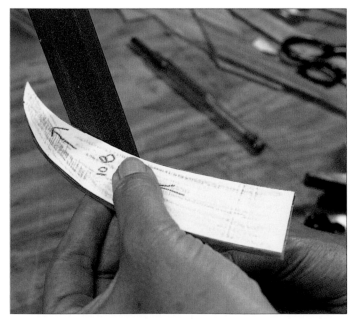

10. Smooth the edges of each cut piece with a carborundum stone or a piece of emery cloth.

11. Or use an electric grinder to smooth the edges. Keep the pattern pieces attached to the glass as you work on the edges.

Step 3 • Assemble the Project

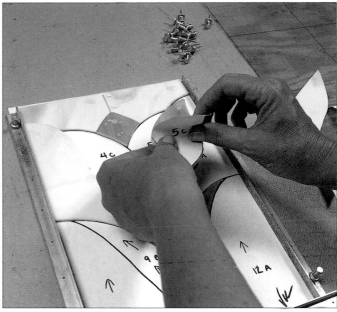

1. Set up your work space by first placing the intact pattern on the surface. Your glass pieces will be assembled on top of this pattern. Place the squaring bars around three sides of the intact copy of your pattern. Use a triangle to be sure the bars are perfectly square. Leave one end open for moving the pieces in and out.

2. Working one piece at a time, remove the pattern template from the cut glass piece and position the piece over the appropriate part of the pattern.

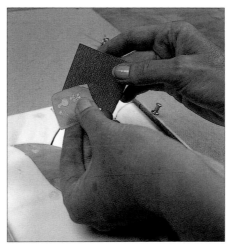

3. Continue positioning until all pieces are in place.

4. If the pieces are too tight or don't fit well, use a piece of emery cloth or an electric grinder to work on the edges and reduce the size of the piece.

5. When all pieces are fitted and placed, add the last squaring bar and secure in place. Leave the pieces within the squaring bars during the foiling process, picking up only one piece at a time to apply the foil. Otherwise, the pieces might not fit together.

Step 4 • Foil the Glass Pieces

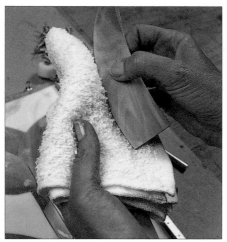

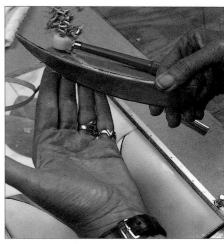

1. Wipe the edges of each glass piece with a cloth to remove any oil residue from the glass cutter and all the powder from the grinder or carborundum stone before you wrap the piece with foil tape. *Option:* Use window cleaner spray, if needed, to remove adhesives or oils.

2. Pull the backing paper from the end of the roll of foil tape and position the edge of the glass piece on the foil, centering the edge of the glass piece on the tape.

3. Keep applying foil tape around the piece to cover ALL the edges of the piece. Keep the piece centered on the foil so the foil overlaps the piece equally on both sides. (This is the easiest part of doing stained glass. If you're making a big project like a lampshade, you may have to apply foil to as many as a thousand pieces – it's time consuming, but not difficult.)

4. When all the edges of a piece have been covered and you get to the place where you started, overlap the foil tape slightly – about 1/4" – and cut the end of the foil tape with a craft knife.

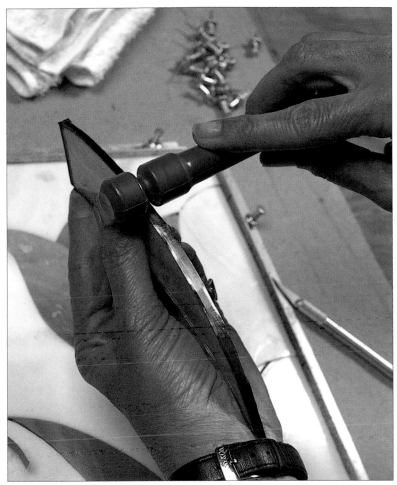

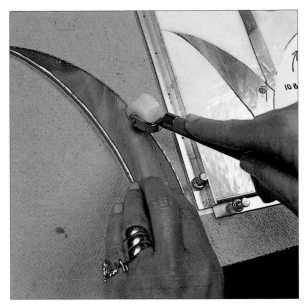

6. Burnish the tape to the sides of the glass piece to secure the foil, using the roller end of the burnisher. Be sure to burnish both sides of the glass piece. If you have done a good job, you won't be able to see where you overlapped the beginning and end of the foil and you won't be able to feel a ridge between the glass and the foil. It should be perfectly smooth on the edges.

5. Burnish the tape on the edge of the glass for a smooth, secure bond by running the grooved end of the burnisher around the edge of the glass to press the tape securely against the edge. **Don't** run your fingers along the edge of the glass – that's a good way to get a foil cut.

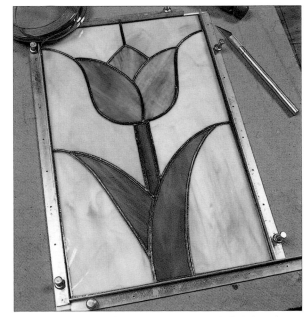

7. Continue the foiling process until foil has been applied to all pieces. Work one piece at a time, replacing each piece within the squaring bars after you apply the foil tape.

Step 5 • Solder the Glass Pieces

Caution: Always solder in an area with adequate ventilation. Soldering fumes are not healthy to breathe.

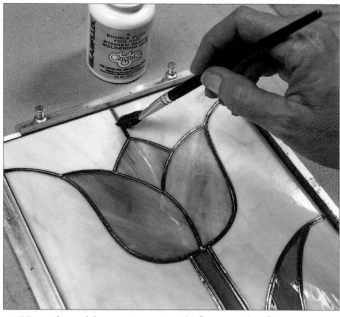

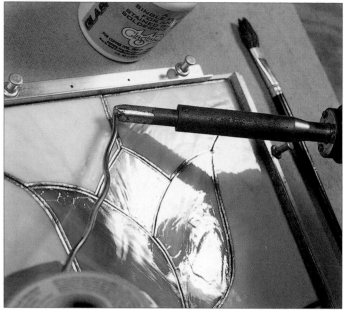

1. Heat the soldering iron. Brush flux on the first area you plan to solder. You do not have to be precise – just make sure you cover the foil. It is okay if you get some flux on the glass.

2. Position the tip of the soldering iron over the foiled area, holding the iron in one hand and the roll of solder in the other hand. Hold the solder wire against the iron to melt the solder as you move the iron along.

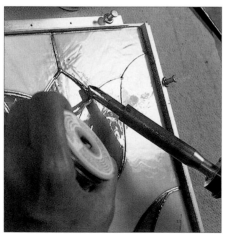

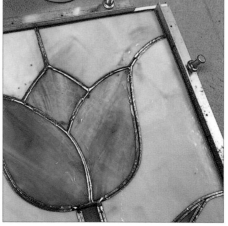

3. Draw the tip of the soldering iron along the flux-brushed foil, melting solder as you go. The solder will stay on the metal and resist the glass.

4. Continue to solder, working one area at a time – first applying flux, then soldering. For a smooth bead of solder at joints where pieces intersect, run the solder a short way in each direction from the joint.

5. When you've completed one side of the piece, turn it over and solder the other side.

TIP: If you notice drip-through on the other side when you turn over the piece, take a wet cloth and lay it underneath the piece as you work. That will cool the solder more quickly and stop drip-throughs from seeping to the other side.

Step 6 • Frame the Piece

*Panels that are intended for outdoor use are usually stabilized along
the edges with a frame of U-shaped metal came.*

1. When you've finished soldering and have removed the squaring bars, measure each side of the piece to determine how much U-shaped came you need to frame the panel, working clockwise. Add the measurements together for each side to get a measurement for the total length of came needed. For example, if you have an 8" x 10" panel, you will need a piece of came 36" long (8" + 8" + 10" + 10").

2. Mark each measurement **in order – working clockwise** on a length of U-shaped came with a felt-tip marker. The marks indicate where the came will be notched so the piece of came will fold around the edges of the panel, forming mitered corners. For example, for an 8" x 10" vertical piece – mark 8", then 10", then 8", then 10".

3. Notch the came at the places you have marked, using a came notcher or a hacksaw.

4. Place the U-shaped came around the panel, bending the came at the notches and positioning the notches at the corners. Use push pins to hold the came in place around the panel.

5. Brush flux on the joint where the two ends of the came come together at one corner. Solder the joint. When you have soldered one side, turn over the panel and solder the joint on the other side.

6. **Option:** You can create little eyes of wire for hanging your panel. Use needlenose or roundnose pliers to form circles of copper or aluminum wire. Solder a wire circle at each side of the panel on the back. Attach monofilament line through the loops to hang the panel.

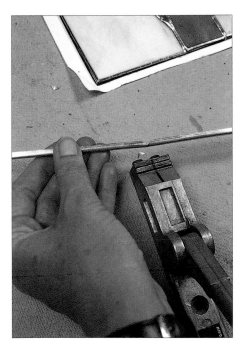

Notching the came for mitering with a came notcher.

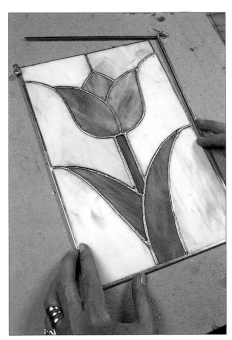

Placing notched came around the edges of the panel.

Soldering the end joint.

All A-Buzz
Glass Mobile

This glass mobile is a constant reminder of the important work honeybees do for us gardeners by pollinating our flowers and vegetables. This project is an easy one. The bees are from a pre-cut kit, and the skep is one piece of glass with copper foil overlays. For a different twist, use the pre-cut kit with a straw bee skep or a metal one cut from tin. I've included a pattern for the bees if you'd like to cut your own.

Size: 8" x 18"

Supplies

1 sq. ft. caramel glass (for skep)
3 pre-cut glass bumblebees *or* 1 sq. ft. *each* iridized white, yellow, and black glass
60/40 solder
Copper foil tape, 7/32" wide
Black patina
Copper wire (for hooks)
Monofilament line (for hanging)

Tools:
Basic tools and supplies (See the beginning of this section for details.)
Glass grinder
Needlenose pliers
Optional: Glass saw

Instructions

See "Crafting with Copper Foil" the beginning of this section.

Prepare:
1. Enlarge your pattern to the desired size. Number each pattern piece. Make a copy of your pattern using a copy machine or trace a copy using carbon paper.
2. Using your pattern shears, cut out one copy of the pattern. Use a craft knife to trim off the outer edges of the other copy.

Cut:
1. Adhere your pattern pieces to the glass using rubber cement.
2. *If you are not working with pre-cut bees,* cut out all glass pieces for the bees.
3. Use a glass saw to cut out the bee skep.

If you don't have a glass saw, cut the skep shape by hand and use the 1/8" grinder bit on your glass grinder to create the deeper inside cuts that create the curves of the skep.
4. Use a glass grinder or grozing pliers to smooth off all the edges and any excess glass from around the pattern template.

Assemble the Bees:
1. Lay out the other copy of the pattern on your work board. Use metal push pins to hold the pattern and the glass pieces in place. When you are happy with the fit, clean any dust or oil off the glass pieces, using a dry cloth.
2. Wrap each glass piece in copper foil. Use your burnisher to adhere the foil tightly to the front, outside edge, and back of each glass piece.

Add Copper Foil to the Skep:
The skep was created using the copper foil overlay technique. Make sure the glass is completely clean and dry before proceeding.
1. Cut pieces of foil to fit the divisions of the skep as shown on the pattern. Make the foil pieces at least 1/4" longer than your measurement so you can wrap the ends of the foil around the edges of the glass.
2. Working one piece at a time, peel off the backing from the foil and lay the foil strips across the hive to create the horizontal divisions. Secure the foil to the surface and edge of the hive using the roller on the burnisher.
3. Wrap the outer edges of the entire piece with foil tape and burnish to secure.

Solder:
1. To solder the overlay strips, use a small amount of flux and flow the solder bead across the overlay just as you would on a copper foil seam.
2. Solder the bees together.
3. Build up the outside edges of the hive and the bees with additional solder.

Finish:
1. Use copper wire to form three wire hooks for hanging. Solder the hooks to the bottom of the skep.
2. Form three wire hooks for the bees. Solder the hooks to the back side of the bees at the seam where the wings meet the body.
3. Use more copper wire to form the bees' antennae. Solder the antennae on the back of each bee where the bee's head meets the body.
4. Clean the pieces with soap and water and rinse well.
5. Apply black patina. (See "About Patinas" on page 91 or follow the package instructions.)
6. Use fishing line to string and hang your mobile. ❑

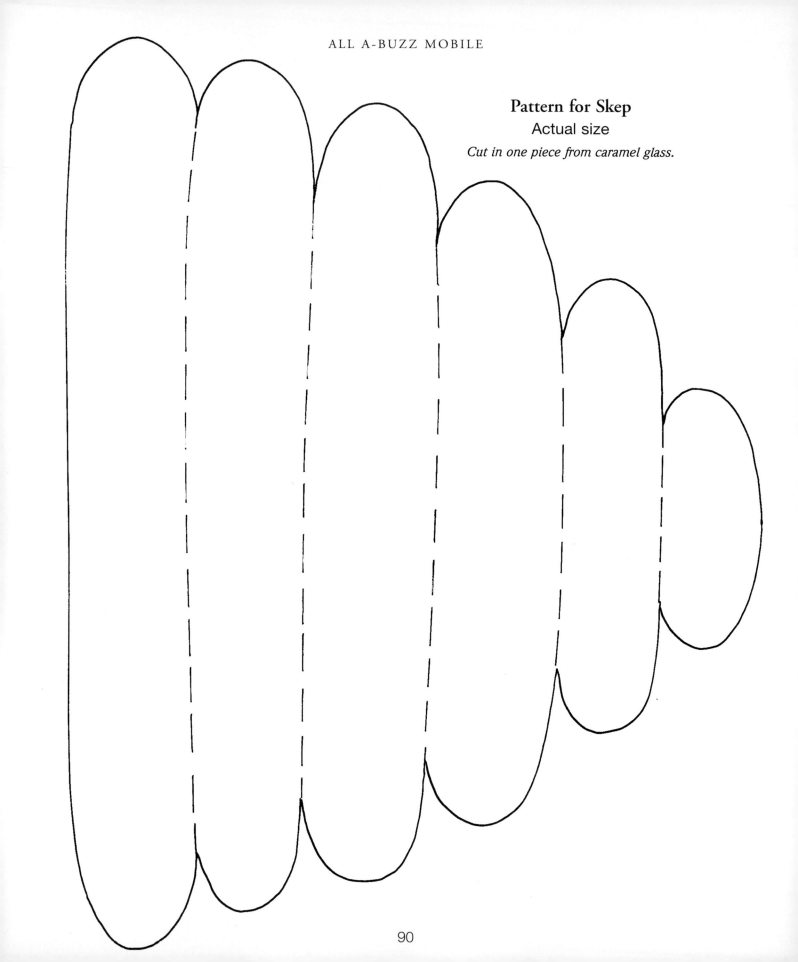

Pattern for Skep
Actual size
Cut in one piece from caramel glass.

Pattern for Bee
Actual size

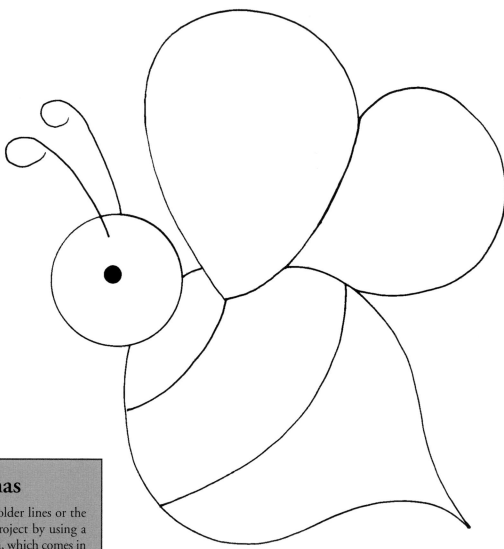

About Patinas

You can change the color of the solder lines or the metal frame on any copper foil project by using a chemical compound called a patina, which comes in black and copper colors. As you apply the patina, try to keep it off the surface of the glass. Patina won't damage the glass – but removing it is another cleanup step you won't need to do if you're careful.

Here's the basic technique:

1. Clean the panel with soap and water.
2. Dip a cotton swab in the patina and carefully paint over the solder lines and the frame. Let the patina remain on the metal for 30 minutes.
3. If a deeper color is desired, apply one or two more coats.

Loves Me, Loves Me Not
Garden Panel

This pretty little daisy answers the age-old questions (Does he love me? Does he love me not?) with a positive, lasting expression of love. I created this white daisy for my true love, but you could change the petal colors to yellow, orange, or even pink.

Panel size: 8" x 10" (You could enlarge this panel by adding a 1" or 2" border of yellow or white glass. If you do, you'll need additional glass and zinc came.)

Supplies

1-1/2 sq. ft. white glass
1/4 sq. ft. green glass
1 sq. ft. aqua glass
Scrap of yellow glass
40" strip of 1/4" U-shaped zinc came
  (for the frame)
Copper wire (for hooks)
60/40 solder
Copper foil tape, 7/32" wide
Optional: Patina

Tools:
Basic tools and supplies (See the
  beginning of this section for
  details.)
Needlenose pliers
Optional: Glass grinder, window
  cleaner spray

Instructions

See "Crafting with Copper Foil" at the beginning of this section.

1. Enlarge the pattern as directed. Number each pattern piece. Make a copy of your pattern using a copy machine or trace a copy using carbon paper.
2. Using your pattern shears, cut out one copy of the pattern. Use a craft knife to trim off the outside edges of your pattern.
3. Adhere your pattern pieces to the glass surface using rubber cement, two-sided tape, or spray adhesive.
4. Cut out all the glass pieces.
5. Use a glass grinder or grozing pliers to smooth off all the edges and remove any excess glass from around the pattern templates.
6. Lay out the other copy of the pattern on your work board. Place the glass pieces on the pattern. Use metal push pins to hold the pattern and glass pieces in place. Make sure you can see the outside of the pattern line around the entire project after you have laid it out. (If you can't, the corners of your finished project will not turn out square or be the size you want it to be.)
7. Once you are happy with the fit, clean any dust or oil off the glass pieces, using a dry cloth. Use a spray window cleaner, if needed, to remove adhesives or oils.
8. Wrap each glass piece in copper foil tape. Use your burnisher to adhere the foil tightly to the front, outside edges, and back of each glass piece.
9. Solder both sides of the panel.
10. Frame the panel with the zinc framing came.
11. *Option:* Apply a patina to the metal parts of the panel and the frame. See "About Patinas" on page 91 for more information.
12. From copper wire, form two wire hooks for hanging. Solder these hooks to the back side of the panel at the top two corners.
13. Clean your panel with soap and water and rinse well. Wipe dry. ❏

Pattern

Enlarge at 110% for
actual size

Pattern

Instructions appear on page 96.

Enlarge at
110% for
actual size

Under the Tuscan Sunflower
Garden Panel

*I fell in love with sunflowers while touring Italy a couple of years ago when
the hills of Tuscany were aglow with acres of these beautiful
flowers and almost every home seemed to welcome me with
these big, bobbing blossoms.
You can have that welcoming greeting at your home with this sunflower
panel. Don't feel like you need to limit yourself to yellow glass — sunflowers come
in all sizes and colors ranging from pale cream petals to deep, rich reds. Select
the colors that lift your spirits and match your entryway.
Hang your panel in an arbor by the front walk or next to the door.*

Pattern is on page 95.

Panel size: 8" x 10"

(You can enlarge this panel by adding a 1" or 2" glass border. If you do, you'll need more glass and more came for framing.)

Supplies

1-1/2 sq. ft. blue glass
1/4 sq. ft. brown textured glass
1/2 sq. ft. green glass
1 sq. ft. *each* of three shades of
   yellow/gold glass
40" strip of 1/4" U-shaped zinc came
   (for the frame)
Copper wire (for hooks)
60/40 solder
Copper foil tape, 7/32" wide
Optional: Black patina

Tools:

Basic tools and supplies (See the
   beginning of this section for
   details.)
Needlenose pliers
Optional: Glass grinder, window
   cleaner spray

Instructions

See "Crafting with Copper Foil" at the beginning of this section.

1. Enlarge the pattern as directed. Number each pattern piece. Make a copy of your pattern using a copy machine or trace a copy using carbon paper.
2. Using your pattern shears, cut out one copy of the pattern. Use a craft knife to trim off the outside edges of your pattern.
3. Adhere your pattern pieces to the glass surface using rubber cement, two-sided tape, or spray adhesive.
4. Cut out all the glass pieces.
5. Use a glass grinder or grozing pliers to smooth off all the edges and remove any excess glass from around the pattern templates.
6. Lay out the other copy of the pattern on your work board. Place the glass pieces on the pattern. Use metal push pins to hold the pattern and glass pieces in place. Make sure you can see the outside of the pattern line around the entire project after you have laid it out. (If you can't, the corners of your finished project will not turn out square or be the size you want it to be.)
7. Once you are happy with the fit, clean any dust or oil off the glass pieces, using a dry cloth. Use a spray window cleaner, if needed, to remove adhesives or oils.
8. Wrap each glass piece in copper foil tape. Use your burnisher to adhere the foil tightly to the front, outside edges, and back of each glass piece.
9. Solder both sides of the panel.
10. Frame the panel with the zinc framing came.
11. *Option:* Apply a patina to the metal parts of the panel and the frame. See "About Patinas" on page 91 for more information.
12. From copper wire, form two wire hooks for hanging. Solder these hooks to the back side of the panel at the top two corners.
13. Clean your panel with soap and water and rinse well. Wipe dry. ❏

Pop-up Daisies
Suncatchers

*Suncatchers are great little works of art. Whether you're using them to brighten
your kitchen window or to bring color and a bit of whimsy to your backyard,
these little daisies are winners.
You add to the impact by making more than one. (Three seems like the perfect number.)
Make them all the same color or mix them up like I did. The stems are created from twisted
copper wire. I added a little curlicue to the end of the wire for fun.*

Flower size: 4" x 7-1/2"

Supplies

For three daisies
1/2 sq. ft. each of white, orange,
  yellow, and lime green glass
1/4 sq. ft. black glass
2 ft. 18-gauge twisted copper wire
  (for the stems)
18-gauge smooth copper wire (for
  hooks)
60/40 solder
Copper foil tape, 7/32" wide
Black patina

Tools:

Basic tools and supplies (See the
  beginning of this section for
  details.)
Needlenose pliers
Optional: Glass grinder, window
  cleaner spray

Safety Tips:
- I keep a pair of disposable garden gloves
  in my studio to wear when I'm tinning
  to protect my hands. I replace them
  after a couple of projects.
- Always wash your hands thoroughly
  after working with metals and chemicals.

Instructions

See "Crafting with Copper Foil" at the beginning of this section.

1. Trace the pattern. Number each pattern piece. Make a copy of your pattern using a copy machine or trace a copy using carbon paper.
2. Using your pattern shears, cut out one copy of the pattern.
3. Adhere your pattern pieces to the glass surface using rubber cement, two-sided tape, or spray adhesive.
4. Cut out all the glass pieces.
5. Use a glass grinder or grozing pliers to smooth off all the edges and remove any excess glass from around the pattern templates.
6. Lay out the other copy of the pattern on your work board. Place the glass pieces on the pattern. Use metal push pins to hold the pattern and glass pieces in place.
7. Once you are happy with the fit, clean any dust or oil off the glass pieces, using a dry cloth. Use a spray window cleaner, if needed, to remove adhesives or oils.
8. Wrap each glass piece in copper foil tape. Use your burnisher to adhere the foil tightly to the front, outside edges, and back of each glass piece.
9. Tin all the pieces individually (see "About Tinning") before starting to assemble the project.
10. Cut three pieces of twisted wire and shape as shown on pattern. Use needlenose pliers to curl the ends of the wire pieces.
11. Lay out the daisy pieces on the pattern on your work board. Secure the pieces with push pins.
12. Lay the wire and two leaves in place. Use masking tape to hold the wire steady. Tack solder all the pieces to each other and to the wire. To tack solder, brush a spot of flux at various points where the pieces touch each other, then solder the spot, effectively "tacking" them together. Use a little more solder when anchoring the leaves to the wire.
13. Solder the daisy pieces together and attach it to the wire. Anchor well with solder.
14. Shape the smooth copper wire to form two hooks for hanging. Solder these hooks at the vertical solder seams on the back of the daisy near the top.
15. Clean each suncatcher with soap and water and rinse well.
16. Apply black patina. See "About Patinas" on page 91 for more information. ❏

Pattern

Actual size

About Tinning

Copper foil tape should be covered with a coating of solder to give it strength and durability. The adhesive on the back of the foil is only there to assist you in applying it, and most of it melts away when you apply heat. When building a foil panel, you solder a "bead" or "seam" that joins the pieces and covers and protects the foil. But in suncatchers and other projects that are not in frames or dimensional projects like boxes, nightlights, and mobiles, it is necessary to coat all the foiled edges with a thin layer of 60/40 solder. This is called "tinning." Tinning is done before the project is assembled.

Here's how:

1. Secure the glass piece to a flame-resistant work surface with metal push pins. (I use Homasote board in my studio – a recycled paper fiberboard used in the construction industry. Look for it at a lumberyard or building supply center in your town.)
2. Coat the foil with flux.
3. Run a hot soldering iron tip coated with a small amount of solder around the top, back and front of each piece, turning the copper from rosy gold to shiny silver. Let cool and proceed with assembly.

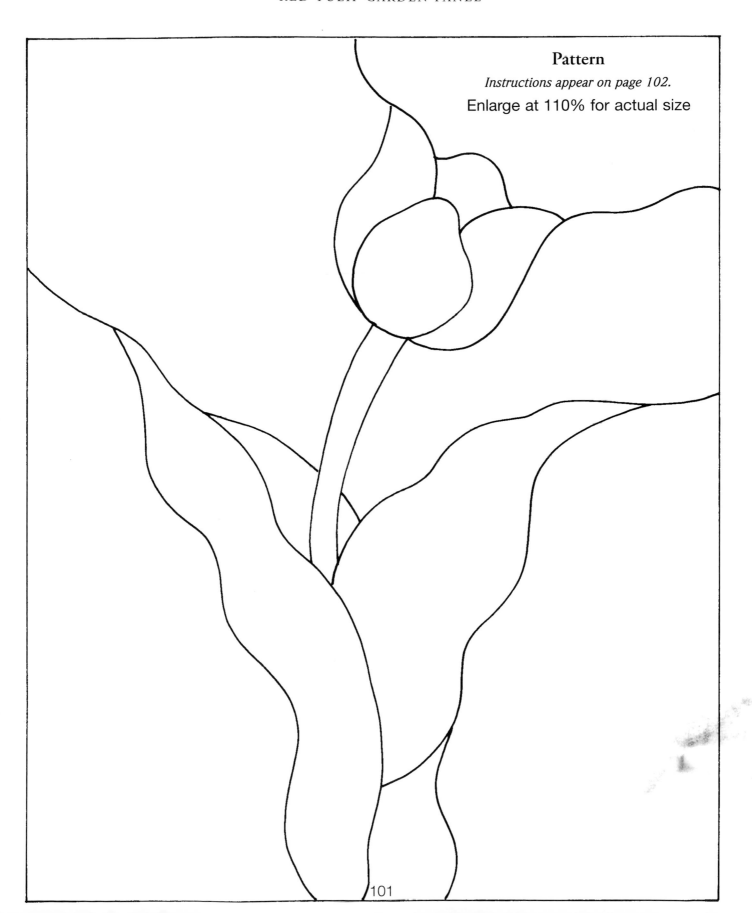

Pattern

Instructions appear on page 102.

Enlarge at 110% for actual size

Red Tulip
Garden Panel

Red is the most spectacular color in the garden, and this red tulip panel makes a colorful accent in the garden any time of year. Pair it in spring with a window box filled with red tulips; in the summer, plant red geraniums.

Pattern is on page 101

Panel size: 8" x 10"
(You can enlarge this panel by adding a 1" or 2" border of red glass. If you do, you'll need more glass and more zinc came.)

Supplies

1-1/2 sq. ft. white frosted glass
1/4 sq. ft. red glass
1/2 sq. ft. spring green glass
40" strip of 1/4" U-shaped zinc came (for the frame)
Copper wire (for hooks)
60/40 solder
Copper foil tape, 7/32" wide
Optional: Patina

Tools:

Basic tools and supplies (See the beginning of this section for details.)
Optional: Glass grinder, window cleaner spray

Instructions

See the "Crafting with Copper Foil" at the beginning of this section.

1. Enlarge the pattern as directed. Number each pattern piece. Make a copy of your pattern using a copy machine or trace a copy using carbon paper.
2. Using pattern shears, cut out one copy of the pattern. Use a craft knife to trim off the outside edges of your pattern.
3. Adhere your pattern pieces to the glass surface using rubber cement, two-sided tape, or spray adhesive.
4. Cut out all the glass pieces.
5. Use a glass grinder or grozing pliers to smooth off all the edges and remove any excess glass from around the pattern templates.
6. Lay out the other copy of the pattern on your work board. Place the glass pieces on the pattern. Use metal push pins to hold the pattern and glass pieces in place. Make sure you can see the outside of the pattern line around the entire project after you have laid it out. (If you can't, your finished project will not turn out square or be the size you want it to be.)
7. Once you are happy with the fit, clean any dust or oil off the glass pieces, using a dry cloth. Use a spray window cleaner, if needed, to remove adhesives or oils.
8. Wrap each glass piece in copper foil tape. Use your burnisher to adhere the foil tightly to the front, outside edges, and back of each glass piece.
9. Solder both sides of the panel.
10. Frame the panel with zinc framing came.
11. *Option:* Apply a patina to the metal parts of the panel and the frame. See "About Patinas" on page 91 for more information.
12. Use copper wire to form two wire hooks for hanging. Solder these hooks to the back side of the panel at the top two corners.
13. Clean your panel with soap and water and rinse well. Wipe dry. ❏

House Numbers
Yard Sign

*Add some curb appeal to your front yard with this easy-to-make yard sign.
You can use a stencil for the numbers or draw them. More advanced
glass workers can substitute their own house in stained glass.
(See the following pages for more information on how to do this.)
In this project, I used an "overlay" technique for the door and the house
numbers. Using overlays allows you to make more detailed-looking projects
with fewer seams.*

Size: 10-1/4" x 9-1/4"

Supplies

2 sq. ft. blue glass
1/2 sq. ft. white glass
1 sq. ft. white iridized (for the
   numbers)
1/2 sq. ft. red glass
1/2 sq. ft. green glass
Scraps of brown and black glass
30 strip of 1/8" U-shaped zinc came
   (for the frame)
2 zinc rods, 1/8" diameter, 18" long
60/40 solder
Copper foil tape, 7/32" wide

Tools:

Basic tools and supplies (See the
   beginning of this section for
   details.)
Optional: Glass grinder, window
   cleaner spray

Instructions

See "Crafting with Copper Foil" at the beginning of this section.

1. Enlarge the pattern to your desired size. Number each pattern piece. Make a copy of your pattern using a copy machine or trace a copy using carbon paper.

2. Using pattern shears, cut out one copy of the pattern. Use a craft knife to trim off the outside edges of your pattern.

3. Adhere your pattern pieces to the glass surface using rubber cement, two-sided tape, or spray adhesive.

4. Cut out all the glass pieces.

5. Use a glass grinder or grozing pliers to smooth off all the edges and remove any excess glass from around the pattern templates.

6. Lay out the other copy of the pattern on your work board. Place the glass pieces on the pattern. Use metal push pins to hold the pattern and glass pieces in place. Make sure you can see the outside of the pattern line around the entire project after you have laid it out. (If you can't, your finished project will not turn out to be the size you want it to be.) The numbers and door are applied as overlays. Set these pieces to the side for now.

7. Once you are happy with the fit, clean any dust or oil off the glass pieces, using a dry cloth. Use a spray window cleaner, if needed, to remove adhesives or oils.

8. Wrap each glass piece in copper foil tape. Use your burnisher to adhere the foil tightly to the front, outside edges, and back of each glass piece.

9. Solder both sides of the panel.

10. Frame the sides and bottom of the panel with zinc came and solder it securely to the panel. Do not continue the frame around the top of the panel – instead, build up the outside edges of the foil with solder as you do when making a suncatcher. (See "About Tinning.")

Continued on page 106

Continued from page 104.

11. Tape the zinc rods to the zinc frame on the sides of the panel. Solder the rods to the zinc frame.

12. Wrap the numbers and the door with foil.

13. Solder the pieces of the numbers together to make the house numbers. Coat the edges of the foil on the numbers and the door with solder. See "About Tinning." Clean the overlay pieces well.

14. Position the numbers and the door on the panel, taping them in place, if needed. Add a dab of silicone glue at the top of the door to hold it in place at top. Apply flux to the contact points (the places where foiled edges touch other foiled edges or the frame) and solder the overlay pieces to the base panel.

15. Clean your panel with soap and water and rinse well. Let dry. ❏

Creating Your Own House in Glass

There are several software programs that can translate any photo or drawing into a stained glass pattern. If you don't have access to one of these programs, here's how to use a photo of your house to create a customized stained glass design:

1. Take a digital photo of your house.

2. Enlarge it to the size you want the house part of your glass panel to be and print a copy.

3. Place tracing paper over the image and trace the basic outline of the house.

   • Simplify the architectural features as much as possible – think cartoon instead of architectural rendering.

   • If you want to add details, consider using wire overlays and full sheets of copper foil to create those details. Full sheets of foil can be cut with a craft knife (much like paper) after it has been applied to the face of the glass. This works great for creating the look of bricks or window muntins.

4. Use the basic outline as your pattern.

Pattern Actual size

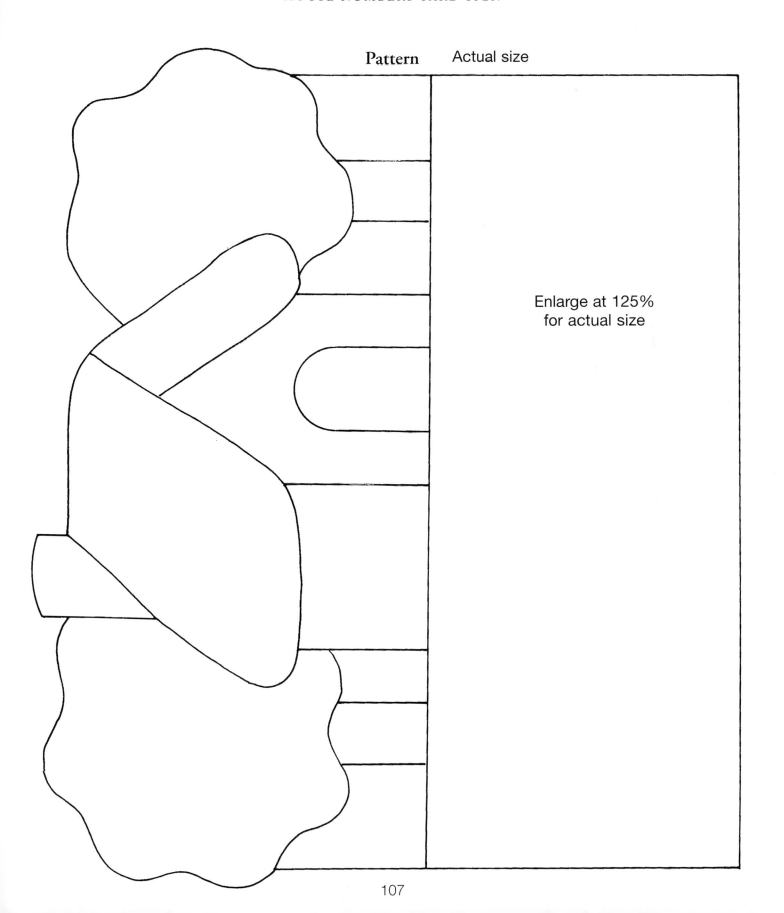

Enlarge at 125%
for actual size

Dragonflies in Flight
Garden Globe

A reflective glass orb allows the whole garden, including the sky, to be viewed with one glance. A single large globe, placed on a stone pedestal, adds elegance to your garden; a wrought iron stand gives strength. I gave the garden globe a new twist by adding beautiful iridized stained glass dragonflies, which I glued to the surface of the globe. You can create this effect on any gazing globe.
You can also add a hanging loop to a glass dragonfly and use it as a suncatcher.
I used pre-cut dragonflies, which are available at craft and glass shops.
A pattern is included if you wish to cut your own.

Dragonfly size: 5" x 6"

Supplies

Glass garden globe
3 pre-cut stained glass dragonflies
1 ft. 18-gauge copper wire
60/40 solder
Copper foil tape, 7/32" wide
Fast-setting glass glue
Painter's tape
Black patina

If you don't use pre-cut dragonflies, for each dragonfly, you'll need:
1/2 sq. ft. white iridized glass
1 medium green glass nugget
7 small blue glass nuggets
Option: Use 5 small blue glass nuggets for the tail and 2 small clear glass nuggets for the eyes

Tools:
Basic tools and supplies (See the beginning of this section for details.)
Needlenose pliers
Paper towels
Optional: Glass grinder, emery cloth, spray glass cleaner

Instructions

The "Crafting with Copper Foil" at the beginning of this section.

Cut the Pieces:
You can skip this section if you're using pre-cut dragonflies.
1. Trace the pattern and number each piece. Make two copies of your pattern using a copy machine.
2. Use scissors to cut out the pattern templates.
3. Affix the wings pattern pieces to the white glass, using rubber cement, two-sided tape, or spray adhesive.
4. Cut out the glass pieces.
5. Use a glass grinder or grozing pliers to smooth off all the edges and any excess glass from around the pattern templates.

Assemble the Dragonflies:
1. Use emery cloth to rub a small band around the edge of each glass nugget to make the foil stick better, or grind a band with the glass grinder.
2. Lay out the other copy of the pattern on your work board. Position the glass pieces on the pattern. Use metal push pins to hold the pattern and glass

Continued on page 110

Caring for Your Globe

- Don't remove or loosen the seal at the neck of the glass ball. The coloration of the ball is on the inside surface of the glass. If moisture gets inside the globe, the reflective color will peel off.
- Gazing globes should be taken inside during the winter months to keep them from freezing and cracking.
- Although rain won't harm the ball in any way, a violent storm could send tree limbs flying and crack the glass.

Continued from pag 108

pieces in place. Shape each dragonfly's body as you like – if each one is a little different, it's more fun.

3. When you are happy with the fit, clean off any dust or oil from the glass pieces using a dry cloth. Use spray window cleaner, if needed, to remove adhesives or oils.

4. Wrap each glass piece in copper foil tape. Use your burnisher to adhere the foil tightly to the front, outside edge, and back of each glass piece.

5. Tin all the pieces individually (see "About Tinning") before starting to assemble the dragonflies.

6. Lay out the dragonfly on the pattern. (Remember to shape each body a little differently. Secure the pieces with push pins.

7. Solder the nuggets together.

8. Working one wing at a time, lift the outside edge of the wing about 1/2" off the work board and solder the wing to the body of the dragonfly. (This gives the look of flight to the dragonfly.) TIP: Use a little more solder than usual when anchoring the wings to the body.

9. To give the dragonfly strength, solder copper wire to the back side of the dragonfly – from one side of one wing, behind the body, and across to the other wing. Hide the wire ends in the solder.

10. Clean up the dragonflies with soap and water and rinse well.

11. Apply black patina according to the patina manufacturer's instructions. See "About Patinas" on page 91 for more information.

Finish:

If you're making a globe:
Using glass glue, attach the dragonflies to the surface of the garden globe. Follow the instructions on the glue package and allow to cure completely before setting the globe outside. TIPS: Use painter's tape to hold them in place while the glue dries. Support the wings during the drying process by gently stuffing paper towels between the wings and the globe.

If you're making a suncatcher:
Use needlenose pliers to make a copper wire loop for hanging. Solder a loop to each dragonfly. ❑

About Garden Globes

Almost forgotten but making a grand re-entry into the garden, the glass gazing ball is rich in history and legend. Known variously as "garden balls," "gazing globes," and "garden globes" in modern times, they have also been called "witch balls," "butler globes," "globes of happiness," and "Victorian balls." Spiritually speaking, peering into the globe is said to provide an experience of oneness with the universe.

The history of the garden globe is as colorful as the ball itself and has its roots in 13th century Venice, Italy, where the early globes were handblown by skilled craftsmen, just as they are today. Antonio Nier, a 15th century priest, called the globe a sphere of light and, as time passed, the colorful ball became a permanent fixture in the European garden and home. Ludwig II, king of Bavaria in the 19th century, adorned his palace, a replica of Versailles, with the globe. Smaller, non-reflective balls made of colored glass were believed to attract and trap evil spirits.

Legends abound concerning the mysterious powers of the reflective ball. A globe was said to bring happiness, good luck, and prosperity to its owner, and to ward off evil spirits, misfortune, illness, and (of all things!) witches. The methods for keeping witches away vary, but all stem from a witch's purported fascination with or fear of her own image. One method involved placing the ball near a house's entrance so if a witch tried to enter, she would be transfixed and so not able to get past her reflection. Other lore maintains that since a witch cannot bear to see her own reflection, she will not come near the witch's ball. Another use of the globe was protection – a witch cannot sneak up on a person gazing into a globe – he or she can see if a witch approaches from behind.

In the garden of the antebellum South, the gazing globe had more practical purposes. Placed strategically by the path from the front gate, people on the veranda could see who was calling before the caller could see them, allowing plenty of time to prepare refreshments for the guest or to hide – whichever was fitting.

In Victorian dining rooms, a reflective butler ball allowed servants to see when guests needed assistance during a meal without looking at them directly. When a ball was placed in the foyer of the home, parents could watch a daughter and her date as he bid her goodnight.

Today, the gazing globe is used as an ornament in the flower garden.

Pattern for Dragonfly

Actual size

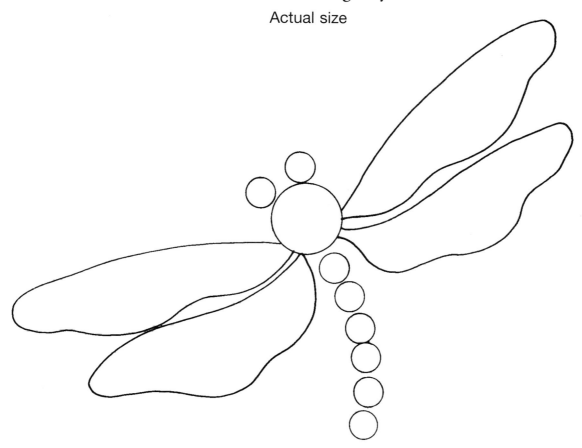

Light Up the Night
Drinking Glass Luminary

You can turn an ordinary drinking glass into a delightful candle holder or vase with wire accents and glass nuggets. It's a great way to recycle any glass with a chipped rim. (I selected a frosted green juice glass for this one.) Try using an old wine glass for a touch of elegance.

Size: 3-1/2" x 4"
(To create a larger candle holder or vase, use a larger glass container. On a larger project, you may want to add more accents.)

Supplies

1 drinking glass or other glass container

60/40 solder

Copper foil tape, 1/4" wide *and* 7/32" wide

18-gauge pre-tinned wire (copper wire with a thin coating of solder already applied)

3 small glass nuggets

Black patina

Tools:
Basic tools and supplies (See the beginning of this section for details.)

Measuring tape

Emery cloth

Instructions

See "Crafting with Copper Foil" at the beginning of this section.

Prepare:
To determine how many and what size wire accents you will need to make, measure the outside circumference of the container and divide that number by three. This will give you the placement locations of the glass nuggets.

Assemble:
1. Apply 1/4" foil to the top edge of the glass. Use your burnisher to burnish, crimp, and smooth the foil tightly to the glass edge.
2. Wrap the three glass nuggets with 7/32" foil. TIP: If you have trouble getting the foil to stick to the nuggets, use a nail file or emery cloth to rough up the edges where you will be adhering the foil.
3. Shape six S-shapes from tinned copper wire to create your accents. Bend the shapes to conform to the top edge of the glass. Use small drops of solder to create beads at the ends of the S-shapes.
4. Tin the nuggets and the edge of the glass. See "About Tinning" for more information.
5. Tack-solder the nuggets in place on the edge of the glass.
6. Tack-solder one of the wire shapes to each side of each nugget and to the edge of the glass.
7. When the three nuggets and six S-shapes are in place, measure the distance between each accent. Cut a piece of straight tinned wire to fit each space.
8. Use small drops of solder to create beads at the ends of the wire pieces and solder in place, using the photo as a guide.
9. Clean the project with soap and water and rinse well.
10. Apply black patina according to the patina manufacturer's instructions. See "About Patinas" on pag 91 for more information. ❑

Garden Cat
Hanging Flag Panel

For centuries cats have been the gardener's friend, chasing away rodents and making us smile when we spot them snoozing on summer afternoons, curled up in a flower pot or a bed of petunias. This stained glass cat flag marks a garden as "cat friendly." If your feline friend isn't a calico, customize the glass colors to your liking.

Panel size: 10" x 10"

Supplies

Metal garden flag pole
2 small S-hooks (to hang the panel)
1 sq. ft. white glass
1 sq. ft. caramel glass
1 sq. ft. black glass
1/2 sq. ft. blue glass
Scraps of yellow glass (for the eyes)
Copper wire (for whiskers and hooks)
40" strip of 1/4" wide U-shaped zinc came (for frame)
60/40 solder
Copper foil tape, 7/32" wide
Outdoor acrylic paints – Black, white
Black patina

Tools:

Basic tools and supplies (See the beginning of this section for details.)
Small paint brush
Needlenose pliers
Optional: Glass grinder, spray window cleaner

Instructions

See "Crafting with Copper Foil" at the beginning of this section.

1. Enlarge the pattern as directed. Number each pattern piece. Make a copy of your pattern using a copy machine or trace a copy using carbon paper.
2. Using your pattern shears, cut out one copy of the pattern. Use a craft knife to trim off the outside edges of your pattern.
3. Adhere your pattern pieces to the glass surface using rubber cement, two-sided tape, or spray adhesive.
4. Cut out all the glass pieces.
5. Use a glass grinder or grozing pliers to smooth off all the edges and remove any excess glass from around the pattern templates.
6. Lay out the other copy of the pattern on your work board. Place the glass pieces on the pattern. Use metal push pins to hold the pattern and glass pieces in place. Make sure you can see the outside of the pattern line around the entire project after you have laid it out. (If you can't, your finished project will not turn out square or be the size you wanted it to be.)
7. Once you are happy with the fit, clean any dust or oil off the glass pieces, using a dry cloth. Use a spray window cleaner, if needed, to remove adhesives or oils.
8. Wrap each glass piece in copper foil tape. Use your burnisher to adhere the foil tightly to the front, outside edges, and back of each glass piece.
9. Solder both sides of the panel.
10. Frame the panel with the zinc framing came.
11. Use copper wire to form two wire hooks for hanging. Solder these hooks to the back side of the panel at the top two corners.
12. To create the cat's whiskers, cut 3" long pieces of copper wire. Coat the wire with solder (so it will accept black patina). **Don't** try to hold them with your fingers – the wire gets hot really fast and you will burn your fingers. Use pliers.
13. Position the wire and secure with masking tape while you tack-solder them in place. Again, **don't** try to hold them with your fingers – the wire gets hot really fast and you could burn your fingers.
14. Clean your panel with soap and water and rinse well. Let dry.
15. Use black patina to turn all the solder, the frame, and the wire black to match the flag pole. See "About Patinas" on page 91 for more information. TIP: If you didn't find black S-hooks, use a little black patina or paint to color them.
16. Use a small paint brush, paint the black and white accents on the eyes, using the photo as a guide.
17. Hang the panel on the pole with S-hooks. ❏

Pattern
Enlarge at 125% for actual size

Pattern courtesy of Spectrum Glass

Pattern

Instructions appear on page 118.

Enlarge at 150% for actual size

Circle of Pansies
Garden Panel

These pansies never need watering and will only look better when the sun shines on them in the summer. The round glass panel is a perfect accent for this trellis with a round opening. The edge of the round panel is accented with twisted lead. This is a fun edging treatment you will enjoy creating.

Pattern is on page 117.

Panel size: 11-1/2" diameter
(You can enlarge this panel by adding a 1" or 2" border of yellow or purple glass.)

Supplies

1-1/2 sq. ft. white glass
1/2 sq. ft. green glass
1 sq. ft. yellow glass
1/4 sq. ft. purple glass
6 ft. 3/16" H-shaped lead came
6 ft. 1/8" U-shaped lead came
Copper wire (for hooks)
60/40 solder
Copper foil tape, 7/32" wide
Black patina

Tools:

Basic tools and supplies (See the beginning of this section for details.)
Power drill
Lead vise or clamp
Needlenose pliers
Optional: Glass grinder, spray window cleaner

Instructions

See "Crafting with Copper Foil" at the beginning of this section.

1. Enlarge the pattern as directed. Number each pattern piece. Make a copy of your pattern using a copy machine or trace a copy using carbon paper.
2. Using your pattern shears, cut out one copy of the pattern. Use a craft knife to trim off the outside edges of the other copy.
3. Adhere your cutout pattern pieces to the glass surface using rubber cement, two-sided tape, or spray adhesive.
4. Cut out all the glass pieces.
5. Use a glass grinder or grozing pliers to smooth off all the edges and remove any excess glass from around the pattern templates.
6. Lay out the other copy of the pattern on your work board. Place the glass pieces on the pattern. Use metal push pins to hold the pattern and glass pieces in place. Make sure you can see the outside of the pattern line around the entire project after you have laid it out. (If you can't, your finished project will not be the size you want it to be.)
7. Once you are happy with the fit, clean any dust or oil off the glass pieces, using a dry cloth. Use a spray window cleaner, if needed, to remove adhesives or oils.
8. Wrap each glass piece in copper foil tape. Use your burnisher to adhere the foil tightly to the front, outside edges, and back of each glass piece.
9. Solder both sides of the panel.
10. Stretch the 1/8" U-shaped lead came by securing one end of the came piece in the vise and pulling gently. Trim the ends and frame the panel with the 1/8" U-shaped lead came. Solder in place.
11. Add the decorative twisted lead edging to the outside of the panel. See "Making Decorative Twisted Lead Edging" for instructions. Secure to the panel with solder.
12. From copper wire, form two wire hooks for hanging. Solder these hooks to the back side of the panel at 2:00 and 10:00.
13. Clean the panel with soap and water and rinse well.
14. Apply black patina to the entire panel, following the patina manufacturer's instructions. See "About Patinas" on page 91 for more information. ❏

Making Decorative Twisted Lead Edging

You will need a power drill and a lead vise or clamp to create this edging. Attach the lead vise to the edge of a table.

1. Insert the lead into the vise – about 2". Push down firmly on the vise lever. Make sure it bites into the lead so the lead won't slip.
2. Insert the other end of the lead came into the drill just as you would a drill bit.
3. Holding the lead out straight, start up the drill – slowly. The lead will start to turn and twist. The longer you run the drill the tighter the twist will

Butterfly & Flower
Patio Box

This colorful stained glass box, accented with a dimensional butterfly and blooming flower, is a beautiful accent for a patio table. It makes a perfect gift for anyone who admires the beauty of nature.

Stained glass boxes are easy to make when you use my fail-proof techniques. I've built hundreds of boxes and accented them with all types of beveled glass pieces, flowers, jewels, and overlays. Once you have made one box, you will be off and running.

Box size: 4" x 6"

Supplies

Green glass, 18" x 6" (for the box)
1/2 sq. ft. yellow glass
1/4 sq. ft. *each* of orange, peach, and lime green glass
1 ft. 20-gauge copper wire (for flower stamen and butterfly antennae)
60/40 solder
Copper foil tape, 7/32" wide
2 brass box hinges
6" box chain
Black patina

Tools:

Basic tools and supplies (See the beginning of this section for details.)
Needlenose pliers
Strip cutter
Optional: Glass grinder, spray glass cleaner

Instructions for Making the Box

See "General Instructions for Making Boxes" on page 122 before you start to cut.

Cut & Assemble:

1. Square up the piece of green glass so all four corners of all pieces are 90-degree angles. Make sure the edges are smooth and straight.
2. Mark the grain of the glass with a felt-tip marker.
3. Set your strip cutter for 2" strips. Cut one 2" x 6" strip of glass for the front of the box. Cut three 2" x 6" strips for the back and sides.
4. To make the shorter sides of the box, cut the side pieces to 4-1/2" long. You can use the strip cutter or cut them by hand.
5. Separate the four box side bottoms (pieces labeled FB, BB, SAB, and SBB in the General Instructions) from the box side tops (pieces labeled FT, BT, SAT, and SBT). Set your strip cutter for 1". Follow the layout and double check the grain markings on the glass before you cut.
6. Cut the top and bottom pieces.
7. Lay out the cut pieces of glass as shown in the General Instructions. Use a grinder to smooth the edges and make adjustments. The edges of each glass piece must be smooth and straight.

Apply Foil & Solder:

1. Wrap all the pieces with 7/32" copper foil.
2. Following the General Instructions, assemble the side top pieces and side bottom pieces of the box and tack-solder. Make sure the top fits easily inside the top sides.
3. Run a smooth solder bead over all inside copper seams. You do not need to solder the outside edges. Turn the lid over and solder the back.
4. To assemble the bottom of the box, wrap the bottom piece in foil and place flat on the work surface, right side up. Place the bottom side section around the bottom. (The bottom should fit easily into the box. Tack-solder the corners of the bottom to the corners of the box. Turn the box over and run a flat, smooth solder seam around the bottom edges, then solder the seams inside the box bottom.

Add Hinges:

1. Fit the top and bottom of the box together. Make sure you are happy with the fit. Secure with two rubber bands to help hold them together while you solder the hinges.
2. Position the hinges on the back of the box. Hold the hinges in place with needlenose pliers. Using a cotton swab or small paintbrush, paint flux on the edge of the hinge. *Tip:* Don't use too much flux or the solder will run into your hinge and ruin it. Remember solder can't travel where there is no flux.

Finish:

1. Solder the front and back outside seams of the box.
2. Solder a length of box chain inside the box to keep the lid from falling backward when opened.

Instructions for Making the Butterfly and Flower Accents

See "Crafting with Copper Foil" at the beginning of this section.

1. Trace and enlarge the patterns. Number each pattern piece. Make a copy of the patterns using a copy machine or trace a copy using carbon paper.
2. Using your pattern shears, cut out one copy of each pattern.
3. Adhere the pattern pieces to the glass using rubber cement, two-sided tape, or spray adhesive.
4. Cut out all the glass pieces.
5. Use a glass grinder or grozing pliers to smooth off all the edges and remove any excess glass from around the pattern templates.
6. Lay out the other copy of the pattern on your work board. Place the glass pieces on the pattern. Use metal push pins to hold the pattern and glass pieces in place.
7. Once you are happy with the fit, clean any dust or oil off the glass pieces, using a dry cloth. Use a spray window cleaner, if needed, to remove adhesives or oils.
8. Wrap each glass piece in copper foil tape. Use your burnisher to adhere the foil tightly to the front, outside edges, and back of each glass piece.
9. Tin all the pieces individually (see "About Tinning" on page 100) before starting to assemble the project.
10. Cut pieces of wire and shape into accents for the flower stamen and antennae for the butterfly. Needlenose pliers work great for curling the wire.
11. Lay out the butterfly wings on the pattern. Secure the pieces with push pins and solder the two wing pieces together on both wings.
12. Place the body of the butterfly on the work board and attach the wings at a slight upward angle to the body. Solder on the antennae.
13. Solder the pieces to make the flower, positioning the petals to create dimension. Add the wire stamen to the flower center.

Continued on next page

Continued from page 121

Instructions for Decorating the Box

1. Clean the butterfly, flower, and box.
2. Apply black patina, following the patina manufacturer's instructions. See "About Patinas" for more information.
3. Position the flower on top of the box and tack-solder in place. TIP: Use a little more solder than usual when anchoring the accents to the box lid.

4. Using the photo as a guide for placement, position the second leaf at the front corner of the box, letting it hang off the corner of the box about 1/2". (The leaf serves as the handle to open and close the box.) Tack-solder in place.
5. Attach the butterfly.
6. Clean up the box with soap and water. Rinse well.
7. Touch up the patina to color the recently soldered spots. ❏

General Instructions for Making Boxes
Use these instructions to create all kinds of stained glass boxes.

This cutting layout (Fig. 1) allows the grain of the glass to flow uninterrupted up the front of the box, across the top, and down the back. If the layout looks strange, just wait – as you assemble the box it will all come together and you will be delighted with the results.

Cutting & Assembling a Box

1. Use a strip cutter to cut the pieces of the box. If you have not worked with a strip cutter before, practice on scrap clear glass before you attempt to cut your art glass.
2. Wrap each piece with copper foil. Assemble and solder the top. Assemble the side pieces and solder at the corners to stabilize.
3. Box pieces are ready for final assembly.

Figure 1:
Cutting layout

| B |
| SBT |
| SBB |
| SAT |
| SAB |
| BB |
| BT |
| T |
| FT |
| FB |

Legend
SBT = Side B Top
SBB = Side B Bottom
SAT = Side A Top
SAB = Side A Bottom
BB = Back Bottom
BT = Back Top
TB = Top Back
TA = Top Front
FT = Front Top
FB = Front Bottom

Pattern for Butterfly

Actual size

Leaf & Petal Pattern

Actual size

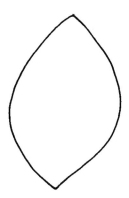

Cut 4 for leaves

Cut 5 for petals

Figure 2: Fitting the box together

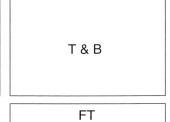

BB

BT

SBB SBT T & B SAT SAB

FT

FB

Figure 3: Placing the pieces together (bird's eye view). Long (front and back) sides are placed inside short sides.

Waving Grass
Candle Holders

To truly admire the beauty of stained glass, illuminate it – the colors come to life when backlit with natural or artificial light. These candle holders are as fun to decorate with as they are to make. By changing the colors of the candles you can coordinate with any decorating scheme. (I selected pink because it works so well with green.)
To create holders for larger-diameter candles, enlarge the diameter of the bottom piece of glass and measure the outside circumference of the circle to determine about how many blades of grass you will need to add to accommodate the increase in size. Make blades of grass shorter or longer, depending upon the height of your candle.

Sizes: Small – 4" x 4", medium – 4" x 6", large – 4" x 9"

Supplies

2 sq. ft. *each* of 3 shades of green glass
60/40 solder
Copper foil tape, 7/32" wide

Tools:
Basic tools and supplies (See the beginning of this section for details.)
Painter's tape
Optional: Glass grinder, glass cleaner spray

Instructions

The steps are the same, regardless of the size of the candle holder. See "Crafting with Copper Foil" at the beginning of this section.

1. Trace the pattern and enlarge as needed. Number each pattern piece. Make two copies of the pattern, using a copy machine.
2. Use scissors to cut out your pattern templates.
3. Affix the pattern pieces to the glass, using rubber cement, two-sided tape, or spray adhesive.
4. Cut out all the glass pieces.
5. Use a glass grinder or grozing pliers to smooth off all the edges and remove any excess glass from around the pattern templates.
6. Lay out the other copy of the pattern on your work board and check the fit of your circle and blades of grass. Once you are happy with the fit, clean off any dust or oil from the glass pieces using a dry cloth. Use a window cleaner spray, if needed, to remove adhesives or oils.
7. Wrap each glass piece in copper foil except for one blade of grass. Use your burnisher to adhere the foil tightly to the front, outside edge, and back of the glass pieces.
8. Tin all pieces individually before you start to assemble the project. See "About Tinning" for more information.
9. Lay out the grass pieces with the right side of the glass down. (The right side is the shinier or smoother side.) Make sure the flat (bottom) edge of the grass pieces are in a straight line. Run a couple of strips of masking tape across the row of grass pieces.
10. Pick up the strip and fit it to the round bottom piece of glass. It should wrap completely around the circumference, leaving no gap between the first blade of grass and the last. If your last grass blade overlaps the first one, use the grinder to reduce the size of the unwrapped grass blade. If it is too small, cut a larger piece to fit. Once the strip of grass blades fits correctly, wrap foil around the last grass piece.
11. Use more masking tape to hold the project together and tack-solder all the pieces to each other and to the bottom disc. Use a little more solder to anchor the grass blades to each other.
12. When you have secured all the pieces with solder, remove the tape. Finish soldering the inside and outside of the candle holder.
13. Clean the candle holder with soap and water and rinse well.
14. Apply black patina, following the patina manufacturer's instructions. See "About Patinas" on page 91 for more information. ❏

Pattern

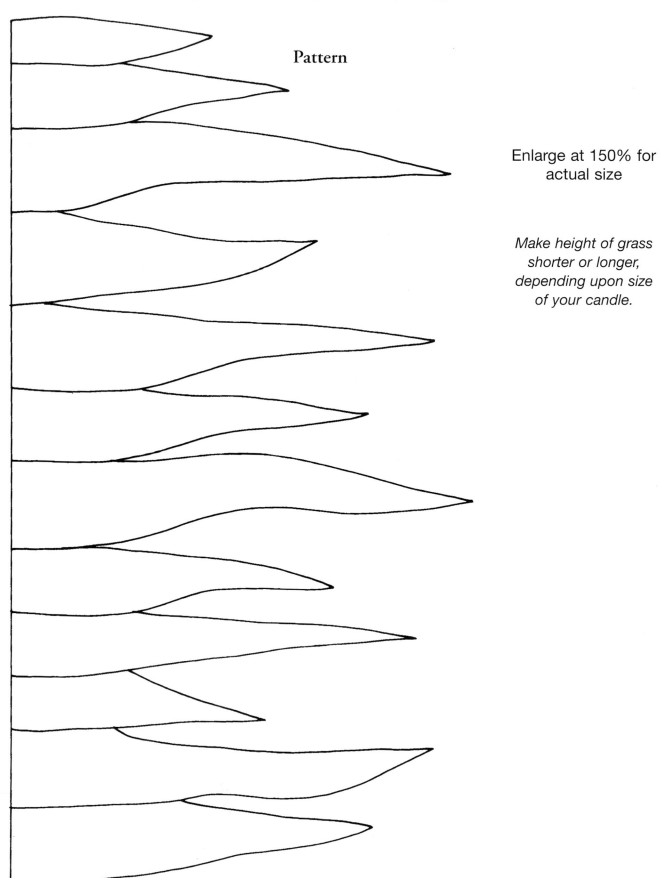

Enlarge at 150% for
actual size

*Make height of grass
shorter or longer,
depending upon size
of your candle.*

Metric Conversion Chart

Inches to Millimeters and Centimeters

Inches	MM	CM	Inches	MM	CM
1/8	3	.3	2	51	5.1
1/4	6	.6	3	76	7.6
3/8	10	1.0	4	102	10.2
1/2	13	1.3	5	127	12.7
5/8	16	1.6	6	152	15.2
3/4	19	1.9	7	178	17.8
7/8	22	2.2	8	203	20.3
1	25	2.5	9	229	22.9
1-1/4	32	3.2	10	254	25.4
1-1/2	38	3.8	11	279	27.9
1-3/4	44	4.4	12	305	30.5

Yards to Meters

Yards	Meters	Yards	Meters
1/8	.11	3	2.74
1/4	.23	4	3.66
3/8	.34	5	4.57
1/2	.46	6	5.49
5/8	.57	7	6.40
3/4	.69	8	7.32
7/8	.80	9	8.23
1	.91	10	9.14
2	1.83		

Index

Index